MW01234913

BAPTISTWAY A[...]

LARGE PRINT EDITION

The Gospel of John

LIGHT OVERCOMING DARKNESS

PART ONE—THE LIGHT SHINES (JOHN 1—12)

BRIAN HARBOUR

BOB DEFOOR

CHARLES GLIDEWELL

JEFF RAINES

WESLEY SHOTWELL

BAPTISTWAYPRESS®

Dallas, Texa[s]

The Gospel of John: Light Overcoming Darkness, Part One, The Light Shines (John 1—12)—BaptistWay Adult Bible Study Guide®—Large Print edition

Copyright © 2010 by BAPTISTWAY PRESS®.
All rights reserved.
Printed in the United States of America.

No part of this book may be used or reproduced in any manner whatsoever without written permission except in the case of brief quotations. For information, contact BAPTISTWAY PRESS, Baptist General Convention of Texas, 333 North Washington, Dallas, TX 75246-1798.

BAPTISTWAY PRESS® is registered in U.S. Patent and Trademark Office.

Scripture marked NIV is taken from The Holy Bible, New International Version (North American Edition), copyright © 1973, 1978, 1984 by the International Bible Society. Used by permission of Zondervan Publishing House. Unless otherwise indicated, all Scripture quotations in lessons 1–8, lessons 12–13, and the Christmas lesson are from the New International Version.

Scripture marked NASB is taken from the 1995 update of the New American Standard Bible®, Copyright © The Lockman Foundation 1960, 1962, 1963, 1968, 1971, 1972, 1973, 1975, 1977, 1995. Used by permission. Unless otherwise indicated, all Scripture quotations in lessons 9–11 are from the New American Standard Bible.

Scripture marked NRSV is taken from the New Revised Standard Version Bible, copyright 1989, Division of Christian Education of the National Council of the Churches of Christ in the United States of America. Used by permission. All rights reserved. Unless otherwise indicated, all Scripture quotations on the back cover, in "Introducing the Gospel of John: Light Overcoming Darkness, Part One, The Light Shines (John 1—12)," and in the unit introductions are from the New Revised Standard Version.

BAPTISTWAY PRESS® Leadership Team
Executive Director, Baptist General Convention of Texas: Randel Everett
Director, Education/Discipleship Center: Chris Liebrum
Director, Bible Study/Discipleship Team: Phil Miller
Publisher, BAPTISTWAY PRESS®: Ross West

Cover and Interior Design and Production: Desktop Miracles, Inc.
                      reproductions Corporation

First edition: December 2010

ISBN-13: 978-1-934731-63-5

How to Make the Best Use of This Issue

Whether you're the teacher or a student—

1. Start early in the week before your class meets.

2. Overview the study. Review the table of contents and read the study introduction. Try to see how each lesson relates to the overall study.

3. Use your Bible to read and consider prayerfully the Scripture passages for the lesson. (You'll see that each writer has chosen a favorite translation for the lessons in this issue. You're free to use the Bible translation you prefer and compare it with the translation chosen for that unit, of course.)

4. After reading all the Scripture passages in your Bible, then read the writer's comments. The comments are intended to be an aid to your study of the Bible.

5. Read the small articles—"sidebars"—in each lesson. They are intended to provide additional, enrichment information and inspiration and to encourage thought and application.

6. Try to answer for yourself the questions included in each lesson. They're intended to encourage further thought and application, and they can also be used in the class session itself.

If you're the teacher—

A. Do all of the things just mentioned, of course. As
   you begin the study with your class, be sure to find a
   way to help your class know the date on which each
   lesson will be studied. You might do this in one or
   more of the following ways:

   • In the first session of the study, briefly overview
     the study by identifying with your class the date
     on which each lesson will be studied. Lead your
     class to write the date in the table of contents on
     page 9 and on the first page of each lesson. *Note*:
     A Christmas lesson is included for the benefit
     of classes who are using this study when first
     published and who wish to study the Christmas
     story itself on the Sunday nearest to Christmas.
     If your class uses the Christmas lesson, you likely
     will need to decide how to study the other lessons,
     such as by combining two lessons or studying the
     missed lesson at a special class meeting.

   • Make and post a chart that indicates the date on
     which each lesson will be studied.

   • If all of your class has e-mail, send them an e-mail
     with the dates the lessons will be studied.

   • Provide a bookmark with the lesson dates.
     You may want to include information about
     your church and then use the bookmark as an

outreach tool, too. A model for a bookmark can be downloaded from www.baptistwaypress.org on the Resources for Adults page.

- Develop a sticker with the lesson dates, and place it on the table of contents or on the back cover.

B. Get a copy of the *Teaching Guide*, a companion piece to this *Study Guide*. The *Teaching Guide* contains additional Bible comments plus two teaching plans. The teaching plans in the *Teaching Guide* are intended to provide practical, easy-to-use teaching suggestions that will work in your class.

C. After you've studied the Bible passage, the lesson comments, and other material, use the teaching suggestions in the *Teaching Guide* to help you develop your plan for leading your class in studying each lesson.

D. Teaching resource items for use as handouts are available free at www.baptistwaypress.org.

E. You may want to get the additional adult Bible study comments—*Adult Online Bible Commentary*—by Dr. Jim Denison (president, The Center for Informed Faith, and theologian-in-residence, Baptist General Convention of Texas). Call 1–866–249–1799 or e-mail baptistway@texasbaptists.org to order *Adult Online Bible Commentary*. It is available only in electronic format (PDF) from our website. See our website, www.baptistwaypress.org, for the price of these comments both for individuals and for a group. A church or class that participates in our advance order program for free shipping can receive *Adult Online Bible Commentary* free. Call 1–866–249–1799 or see www.baptistwaypress.org for information on participating in our free shipping program for the next study.

F. An additional teaching plan is also available in electronic format (PDF) by calling 1–866–249–1799. See our website, www.baptistwaypress.org, for the price of this item both for individuals and for a group. A church or class that participates in our advance order program for free shipping can receive *Adult Online Teaching Plan* free. Call 1–866–249–1799 or see www.baptistwaypress.org for information on participating in our free shipping program for the next study.

G. You also may want to get the enrichment teaching help that is provided on the internet by the *Baptist Standard* at www.baptiststandard.com. (Other class participants may find this information helpful, too.) Call 214–630–4571 to begin your subscription to the printed or electronic edition of the *Baptist Standard*.

H. Enjoy leading your class in discovering the meaning of the Scripture passages and in applying these passages to their lives.

Writers of This Study Guide

Brian Harbour wrote lessons one through three. After serving as a pastor for forty-two years, Dr. Harbour retired to give his attention to writing and teaching. He is president of SeminaryPLUS, a non-profit organization that provides coaching and encouragement to pastors. He also serves as an adjunct professor at Dallas Baptist University and as Visiting Professor in Religion at Baylor University.

Bob DeFoor of Harrodsburg, Kentucky, wrote lessons four through six and the Christmas lesson. Dr. DeFoor served more than forty years as a pastor of churches in Kentucky and Georgia, serving the last twenty-eight prior to retirement as pastor of Harrodsburg Baptist Church. Both Bob and his wife Sandy are native Georgians, and they are graduates of Baylor University. Bob is a veteran writer of Sunday School lessons, and his Sunday School lessons have also been heard on radio for twenty-eight years.

Charles Glidewell wrote lessons seven and eight in the *Study Guide* and "Teaching Plans" for lessons seven and eight in the *Teaching Guide*. He is the pastor of Cross Roads Baptist Church in Rotan, Texas. He received the Master of Divinity degree from Logsdon Seminary, Abilene, Texas.

Jeff Raines, writer of lessons nine through eleven, is associate pastor, First Baptist Church, Amarillo, Texas. Dr. Raines is a graduate of Baylor University, Truett Seminary, and Princeton Seminary (D. Min.). He has served as the second vice president of the Baptist General Convention of Texas (2008).

Wesley Shotwell wrote lessons twelve and thirteen. Dr. Shotwell is pastor of Ash Creek Baptist Church, Azle, Texas. He formerly was pastor of churches in Tennessee. He is a graduate of Baylor University (B.A.), Southwestern Baptist Theological Seminary (M.Div.), and Vanderbilt Divinity School (D.Min.).

The Gospel of John: Light Overcoming Darkness

PART ONE, THE LIGHT SHINES

DATE OF STUDY

UNIT ONE
Signs and Events Showing Jesus' Superiority

UNIT TWO

Signs and Feasts Showing Jesus' Identity

Introducing

THE GOSPEL OF JOHN: Light Overcoming Darkness

PART ONE—THE LIGHT SHINES (JOHN 1—12)

The Gospel of John is many Christians' favorite book of the Bible. It contains wonderful and seemingly simple stories. Here are some of the incidents and passages included in the Gospel of John that are familiar to many Christians:

- Jesus turning water into wine at a wedding (John 2)
- Jesus' conversation with Nicodemus (John 3), which includes one of the most familiar concepts of the Christian faith, being *born again*, and perhaps the most familiar verse in all the Bible, John 3:16
- Jesus' conversation with the Samaritan woman (John 4)
- Jesus as the Good Shepherd (John 10)
- Jesus raising Lazarus from the dead (John 11)
- Jesus washing the disciples' feet (John 13)
- Jesus' statement that he was *going to prepare a place* for his disciples (John 14)

- Jesus' prayer for his disciples (John 17)
- Jesus' appearance to Thomas (John 20)
- Jesus' questioning Peter about whether Peter truly loved him (John 21)

A Closer Look

With so many familiar passages in the Gospel of John, one way of reading and studying the Gospel of John is simply to think of and consider it in light of these passages, passages we may well have known for years. For all the seeming simplicity, though, a closer look at the Gospel of John reveals that it can and should be studied on a deeper level. For one thing, much of the first seventeen chapters of the Gospel of John is unique to it, not appearing in the Gospels of Matthew, Mark, or Luke. Look back at the list in the previous section of familiar incidents and passages. None of those incidents and teachings appear in the other Gospels. They are unique to the Gospel of John. Consider, too, what is often referred to as *the prologue* of the Gospel of John, John 1:1–18. Nothing like it appears in any of the other Gospels.

Of course, we see some familiar incidents in John's Gospel that also appear in one or more of the other Gospels—Jesus feeding the 5,000, for example (John 6)—but even this incident is handled differently and interpreted in much greater depth and detail than in the other

Gospels. Only when we get to Jesus' trial, crucifixion, and resurrection do we find ourselves moving in territory that seems familiar because of our study of the other Gospels. Even here, though, comparing John to the other Gospels shows John's special approach.

The Gospel of John is structured uniquely, too. Many New Testament students have observed that the Gospel of John splits fairly neatly into two major parts. John 1—12 is often referred to as *the Book of Signs*. The second major part of the Gospel is John 13—21. In this portion, John 13—20 is referred to as *the Book of Glory*, with John 21 as an epilogue.

Consider another word about this Gospel's uniqueness, especially in John 2—12. Were it not for the Gospel of John, we would not know of Jesus' extensive ministry in Jerusalem earlier than the week of his death. Indeed, we would not even know of the likelihood of a three-year ministry of Jesus. The timeline of the other Gospels can be put into a single year, while John alone mentions three Passovers (see 2:13; 6:4; 11:55).

The Theme of the Gospel of John

One way to state the theme of the Gospel of John is to combine the thoughts of John 1:5, "The light shines in the darkness, and the darkness did not overcome it," and 1:11, "He came to what was his own, and his own people did not accept him." So the title of the first part of the Gospel, John 1—12, could be stated as *The Light Shines*, and the title of the second part, John 13—21, as *The Light Overcomes*. The Gospel of John is thus the story of *Light Overcoming Darkness*.

The First Part of the Gospel of John

Consider the first part of the Gospel for now. The prologue appears in John 1:1–18, followed by the account in John 1:19–51 that centers on John the Baptist and how several of his disciples gravitated to Jesus. Read John 2 and you will see the first mention of Jesus' signs. Referring to Jesus' turning the water into wine, John 2:11 states, "Jesus did this, the first of his signs, in Cana of Galilee, and revealed his glory; and his disciples believed in him." Thus begins an emphasis in this portion of the Gospel on "signs."

Many students of the Gospel of John consider John 2—12 to be organized around *seven* signs, as follows:

(1) Jesus turning the water into wine (2:1–11)
(2) Jesus healing the son of the royal official (4:46–54)
(3) Jesus healing the paraplegic (5:1–18)
(4) Jesus feeding the 5,000 (6:1–14, 25–69)
(5) Jesus walking on the water (6:16–21)
(6) Jesus restoring the sight of the blind man (9:1–41)
(7) Jesus raising Lazarus to life (11:1–44)

These seven signs should be thought of as *examples* of Jesus' signs rather than as being *all* the signs Jesus did. Jesus did other signs (see 2:23).

The specific word "sign" is used in the Scripture passages telling about five of these incidents (2:11; 4:54; 6:14; 9:16; 12:18). The other incidents appear to have the similar character of a "sign," too. The theme of "signs" is also apparent in other places in the Gospel of John (see 2:23; 3:2; 6:26; 7:31; 10:41; 11:47; 12:37; 20:30).

So signs showing Jesus' identity are emphasized in the Gospel of John, especially chapters 2—12. There's more. Read these chapters with care, and you may see that the Gospel of John has something additional in mind. An important feature of the Scripture passages in these chapters, especially John 2—4 (studied in unit one), is that they show how Jesus, God's Son, signified his identity by superseding various Jewish rituals and institutions— purification practices (John 2); the temple (John 2); the learning of the rabbis (John 3); and all sacred places (John 4). John 2—12 also contrasts mere *signs-faith* and genuine faith.

In addition, the Gospel of John teaches about Jesus by referring to various Jewish festivals. The festivals that appear in the first half of the Gospel of John include the Sabbath (John 5); Passover (2:13–25; 6:1–71; see also 12—20); Booths (also known as Tabernacles, John 7—9); and Dedication (*Hanukkah,* 10:22–39).

As we study these chapters, take note of how in the Gospel's treatment of each of these—the signs, the festivals, and the rituals and institutions—we see Jesus standing out more and more clearly. As he does, he reveals more and more who he is, "the Word" who "became flesh" (1:18), and thus worthy of believing in him as "the Messiah, the Son of God" so that "through believing you may have life in his name" (20:31).

The Second Part of the Gospel of John

The second major part of the Gospel of John, chapters 13—21, deals with Jesus in the last week of his earthly life and then in a week and an additional short amount of time beyond. John 13—17 focuses on Jesus and the disciples in the upper room. Then chapters 18—19 treat Jesus' trial and crucifixion. Chapters 20—21 deal with four resurrection appearances of Jesus.

Our Study of the Gospel of John

Because of the richness, depth, unique structure, and length of the Gospel of John, we are studying it in two parts, two volumes, and devoting more lessons to it than normal. This Gospel's general popularity with Bible students also encouraged our doing this more extensive and more in-depth study.

Since the beginning of our BaptistWay adult Bible study series, we have focused on the Gospel of John twice previously. (This study appears in our eleventh year of publishing Bible study materials.) The first study, *The Gospel of John: So That You May Believe*, is available only in downloadable PDF format since it is no longer in print. The second study, different from the first, is titled *The Gospel of John: The Word Became Flesh*. It is still in print as well as being available in PDF. Each of these studies is thirteen lessons long.[1] This study, though, is being planned for twenty-four sessions, with thirteen in this volume and eleven in another.

Obviously, the Gospel of John for all its simplicity is a rich book for study. It is at once both simple and complicated. But how could we expect otherwise? After all, the subject of the Gospel of John is God becoming flesh in a human being, Jesus. Not only that, it is the account of this human being, Jesus, in whom God was uniquely present, giving his life and being rejected by "his own people" (1:11). What kind of God is this? How could this happen? The Gospel of John calls us to ponder such questions rather than merely to consider interesting stories, sayings, and structure.

A brilliant Baptist interpreter of the Gospel of John, George Beasley-Murray,[2] suggested that the Gospel of

John can speak to people in various life situations. New believers can find in John a wonderful exposition of the faith they have embraced. Mature Christians can continue to find their faith illumined as they learn more of Jesus through this Gospel. Aged Christians can learn even more of the glory of God as it is revealed in this Gospel. Those who are dying can find comfort in its words that tell of Jesus' bringing peace, comfort, and hope.

Let us add that those who have not yet believed can be led to believe through a study of this Gospel. As the Gospel of John states, "Jesus did many other signs in the presence of his disciples, which are not written in this book. But these are written so that you may come to believe that Jesus is the Messiah, the Son of God, and that through believing you may have life in his name" (20:30–31).

Which vantage point is yours? Whatever the case, as you study this Gospel, let John's message speak to you.

Note: The time of the first release of these materials includes the Christmas season. To meet the needs of churches who wish to study the familiar Christmas story from Matthew or Luke at this time, a Christmas lesson is included. If you use the Christmas lesson during this time, plan carefully how you will study the lesson in the Gospel of John if you wish the class to study John 20:1–18 on Easter. Try not to skip a lesson on this Gospel, but perhaps schedule an extra class session around a fellowship time.

Additional Resources for Studying the Gospel of John[3]

George R. Beasley-Murray. *John.* Word Biblical Commentary. Volume 36. Second edition. Waco, Texas: Word Books, Publisher, 1999.

Raymond E. Brown. *The Gospel According to John (I—XII).* Garden City, New York: Doubleday & Company, Inc., 1966.

Raymond E. Brown. *The Gospel According to John (XIII—XXI).* Garden City, New York: Doubleday & Company, Inc., 1970.

F.F. Bruce. *The Gospel of John.* Grand Rapids, Michigan: William B. Eerdmans Publishing Company, 1983.

Gary M. Burge, *The NIV Application Commentary: John.* Grand Rapids, Michigan: Zondervan Publishing House, 2000.

James E. Carter. *John.* Layman's Bible Book Commentary. Volume 18. Nashville: Broadman Press, 1984.

Herschel H. Hobbs. *The Gospel of John: Invitation to Life.* Nashville, Tennessee: Convention Press, 1988.

William E. Hull. "John." *The Broadman Bible Commentary.* Volume 9. Nashville, Tennessee: Broadman Press, 1970.

Craig S. Keener. *The Gospel of John: A Commentary.* Two volumes. Peabody, Massachusetts: Hendrickson Publishers, 2003.

Lesslie Newbigin. *The Light Has Come: An Exposition of the Fourth Gospel.* Grand Rapids, Michigan: William B. Eerdmans Publishing Company, 1982.

Gail R. O'Day. "The Gospel of John." *The New Interpreter's Bible.* Volume IX. Nashville, Tennessee: Abingdon Press, 1995.

N O T E S

1. See www.baptistwaypress.org.

2. George R. Beasley-Murray, *John*, Word Biblical Commentary, vol. 36 (Waco, Texas: Word Books, Publisher, 1987), x. Dr. Beasley-Murray taught the New Testament in both the United States and Great Britain and is now gone to be with the Lord of whom this Gospel is written.

3. Listing a book does not imply full agreement by the writers or BAPTISTWAY PRESS® with all of its comments.

Signs and Events Showing Jesus' Superiority to Judaism's Institutions

This unit treats John 1—4. It provides a study of the prologue (John 1:1–18); Jesus' sign at the wedding in Cana (2:1–11); Jesus' cleansing the temple (2:13–22); Jesus' conversation with "a Teacher of Israel" who yet did not understand (3:1–16); Jesus' conversation with the Samaritan woman (John 4:1–42); and Jesus' "second sign" in Cana (4:46–54).

An important feature of the Scripture passages in this unit, especially John 2—4, is that they show how Jesus, God's Son, signified his identity by showing himself superior to and superseding various Jewish rituals and institutions. These rituals and institutions include purification practices (John 2); the temple (John 2); the learning of the rabbis (John 3); and all sacred places (John 4). This unit also contrasts mere *signs-faith* and genuine faith.[1]

UNIT ONE. SIGNS AND EVENTS
SHOWING JESUS' SUPERIORITY

Lesson 1	God Living Among Us	John 1:1–18
Lesson 2	Jesus Revealing His Glory	John 2:1–11
Lesson 3	Jesus' Authority as Son of God	John 2:13–25
Lesson 4	The Smartest, Most Religious Person in the Room	John 3:1–16
Lesson 5	The Source of Fulfillment	John 4:4–30, 39–42
Lesson 6	*Signs-Faith* or True Faith?	John 4:46–54

N O T E S

1. Unless otherwise indicated, all Scripture quotations in unit 1, lessons 1–6, are from the New International Version.

LESSON ONE
God Living Among Us

MAIN IDEA

In Jesus the eternal Word became flesh, uniquely revealing God and enabling those who trust in him to become God's children.

QUESTION TO EXPLORE

Who is Jesus?

STUDY AIM

To explain the significance for our world and my life of who Jesus is

QUICK READ

God's becoming flesh in Jesus reminds us that God is a God who is with us as well as a God who is majestic and separated from us.

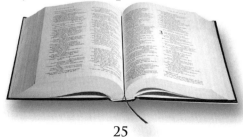

We had a failure in communication. Like most people, you probably can imagine a time when some problem occurred in human relationships because of a failure in communication. With the most important message of all to communicate, John wanted to be sure there was no failure in communication.

The world to which John wrote his Gospel was Greek in character and in its patterns of thought. John wanted to communicate the story of Jesus, which was lived out in a Jewish culture, to a world that was largely ignorant of Hebrew thought patterns. John used the term *Logos* or *the Word* to accomplish that monumental feat.

The idea of the Word had deep roots in Greek thought. To the Greeks, the Word provided the basis for order and continuity in a world of change. The Word was the mind of God that penetrated the universe to give it coherence. It was the tiller by which God, the pilot of the universe, steered all things.

At the same time, the *idea* of the Word was deeply rooted in Hebraic thought. In Hebrew thought, the Word was the sovereign energy that called the created order into being (Psalm 33:6–9). The Word was the omnipotent power that could accomplish the divine purpose (Isaiah 55:11). The Word was the revealed wisdom that could teach people about God (Ps. 119).

So the Word was a concept with which both the Jews and the Greeks were familiar. John said to both of these groups that the Word came to earth in the person of Jesus Christ. John developed this idea of the Word in the opening chapter of his Gospel.

JOHN 1:1–18

1 In the beginning was the Word, and the Word was with God, and the Word was God. **2** He was with God in the beginning.

3 Through him all things were made; without him nothing was made that has been made. **4** In him was life, and that life was the light of men. **5** The light shines in the darkness, but the darkness has not understood it.

6 There came a man who was sent from God; his name was John. **7** He came as a witness to testify concerning that light, so that through him all men might believe. **8** He himself was not the light; he came only as a witness to the light. **9** The true light that gives light to every man was coming into the world.

10 He was in the world, and though the world was made through him, the world did not recognize him. **11** He came to that which was his own, but his own did not receive him. **12** Yet to all who received him, to those who believed in his name, he gave the right to become children of God— **13** children born not of natural descent, nor of human decision or a husband's will, but born of God.

14 The Word became flesh and made his dwelling among us. We have seen his glory, the glory of the One and Only, who came from the Father, full of grace and truth.

15 John testifies concerning him. He cries out, saying, "This was he of whom I said, 'He who comes after me has surpassed me because he was before me.'" **16** From the fullness of his grace we have all received one blessing after another. **17** For the law was given through Moses; grace and truth came through Jesus Christ. **18** No one has ever seen God, but God the One and Only, who is at the Father's side, has made him known.

The Preexistence of the Word (1:1–5)

John began his Gospel, not in the historical context of John the Baptist's preaching (as in the Gospel of Mark) or with Jesus' historic lineage (as in Matthew and Luke) but at the beginning of time. John declared the living Word had existed forever. He explained that "The Word was with God" (John 1:1). The phrase "with God" means *eye-to-eye* or *face-to-face* and signifies equality between God and the Word.

Next John shifted from divine equality to personal identity with the claim that "the Word was God" (1:1). This phrase suggests that the Word was of the very same character and quality of God. The first significant fact about the living Word, which John's Gospel later identified with Jesus, was that he was with God from the beginning and that he is equal to God.

John described this pre-existent Word with two concepts: life and light. Like Paul in his Epistle to the Colossians (Colossians 1:16), John pictured Jesus as the central force behind creation. John concluded: "In him was life" (John 1:4). John also identified Jesus with the term "light." The creation story seems to be in the background of John's use of this image. God eclipsed the darkness with his simple word: "Let there be light" (Genesis 1:3). In the same way, Jesus eclipsed the darkness of the world with the force of his life. John concluded that "that life was the light of men" (John 1:4).

What kind of impact does light in Christ have on the darkness of this world? John said that the darkness "has not understood it," that is, the light that is Christ (1:5). The Greek word translated "understood" literally means *to lay hold of something* and can mean *to understand* in a figurative sense. In a more literal sense, the phrase can mean *to seize something.* The verse could be translated: *The light shines in the darkness, and the darkness has not been able to put it out.* This is John's conclusion: the world could not completely comprehend or ultimately overcome the light that illuminated the world's darkness when the preexistent Word broke into our world.

The Proclamation of the Word (1:6–9)

The author of the Fourth Gospel changed from his focus on the Word to one of the most unusual personalities in the New Testament, John the Baptist. Personal details about John are sparse in this account. The author did not tell us of John the Baptist's miraculous conception or that he was Jesus' cousin. He did not tell us John baptized Jesus or that John wore the garment of the prophet or that he ate the diet of the desert hermit. He did not display the brashness of John's confrontational method. He did not tell us the details of John the Baptist's successful evangelistic campaign or disclose the details of his death. All of those details are in Matthew, Mark, and Luke—the three Gospels known as the Synoptic Gospels. All we see in today's text is this simple declaration about John: "He came as a witness to testify concerning that light" (1:7).

A light came into the world of darkness, a light that the world's darkness could neither comprehend nor extinguish. John the Baptist was not that light. Instead, his purpose was to identify that light. John was not to call attention to himself but rather to bear witness to that light (1:7). Throughout his ministry, John the Baptist fulfilled that purpose. Here at the beginning of his ministry, John the Baptist turned the attention of the crowd away from himself by pointing to the one whom he identified as the light of the world (1:29, 36). The author consistently highlighted Jesus' superiority over John the Baptist (3:22–26;

5:33–36; 10:40–42). John the Baptist pointed to Jesus and testified that Jesus was the one who came from God to meet the needs of humanity.

The Presence of the Word (1:10–14)

John resumed his focus on the Word and announced that the Word "became flesh and made his dwelling among us" (1:14). He explained that "the Word became flesh" [Greek: *sarx*]. John did not mean that God simply took on a human body. The word for body in the Greek is *soma*, but John did not use that word. Instead, he employed the word *sarx*, which, as John used it, includes our body, mind, soul, and moral nature. Paul used the term *sarx* to denote the sinful nature of humanity, but John used it in a more inclusive sense. *Sarx* includes everything that makes a human, human. It means that God became one of us. In Jesus, humanity in all its finiteness and God in all his infinitude came together as one.

That God became human is difficult to conceptualize. Yet, as difficult as it is to conceptualize, the truth of the incarnation must nevertheless be declared.

Two false ideas constantly challenge our understanding of Jesus. One humanizes him to the degree that his divinity is lost. The other deifies him to the degree that his humanity is lost. The incarnation guards against both misconceptions. We can never understand Jesus in any way that implies he is less than or inferior to God. Neither can we understand Jesus if we fail to realize that in all ways he was as human as we are.

John added that the Word "made his dwelling among us." This phrase pictures someone pitching a tent or a tabernacle. In Jesus, God *tabernacled* among us. In the tabernacle of flesh and blood we call Jesus, a new truth exploded in human history, the daring declaration that God is here in our midst.

Each of us has to choose how we will respond to the incarnate Word of God. Some choose to ignore him, not recognizing who he is. Others choose to reject him because he does not fit their stereotype of what God should look like. Some, however, recognize him and receive him. God identifies those who choose to receive Jesus as his children (1:12–13). John clearly acknowledged that our rebirth as children of God does not come from human relationships or from human achievement (1:13). We are children of God because of God's transforming act of grace activated in us by our faith.

The Preeminence of the Word (1:15–18)

The author of the Fourth Gospel again turned his attention to John the Baptist, whose primary concern was to highlight Jesus. John the Baptist acknowledged his own insignificance in comparison to Jesus (1:15). To fully appreciate John's deference to Jesus, we need to see it against the backdrop of the popular response to John's ministry and the unique power attributed to him by adoring crowds. John the Baptist was basking in the glory of his popular wilderness preaching ministry. In his mind, however, his temporary glory paled when compared to Jesus' pre-eminent and permanent power.

The author also acknowledged the insignificance of the law in comparison to Jesus (1:16–17). To fully appreciate the significance of this comparison, we need to place it in the Jewish context of that day when nothing was considered to be more important than the law of God. The law provided the justification for Israel's sense of superiority, and it provided the understanding of God and the guidelines for living that enabled the Jewish people to maintain that sense of superiority. The benefits of the law and the understanding of God communicated through the law, however, paled in significance when contrasted to the benefits of God's grace available through Jesus and with the revelation of God given through Jesus Christ.

In this opening chapter in his Gospel, John bracketed his remarkable Christology with two themes: (1) Jesus' identity with God, reflected in the concept of the Word; and (2) Jesus' identity with humanity, reflected in the concept of incarnation. In these dual themes, John reminded his listeners that God is not only *out there*, the omnipotent Creator of all things; he is also *here in our midst*, the available companion to all people.

Applying This Lesson to Life

What lessons do we learn from our text? To begin with, our text reminds us that Jesus is trustworthy. The Jews put their trust in the preaching of the prophets, the truths of the Torah,[1] and the traditions of the patriarchs. The Greeks put their trust in physical prowess and intellectual development. We today put our trust in money, security, and power. Because Jesus' life is rooted in the very being of God, he above all other authorities is worthy of our trust. We can count on him.

Our text also reminds us that Jesus is touchable. Jesus does not stand apart from us. Instead, he is in our midst. He took on flesh and dwelled among us. He is present with us.

When a little girl was told that the church on the corner was God's house, she told her mother, "We are really lucky to live in the same neighborhood with God." Our text affirms that truth. Because this One who was with God in the beginning and who was God who became flesh and dwelled among us, we are living in the same neighborhood with God.

GLORY

The word *glory* appears throughout the Bible. In the Old Testament, the glory (*kabod*) of God is a manifestation of the divine attributes that distinguish him from humanity. In some cases, witnessing the glory of God brought encouragement, as it did to Moses when he asked God to reveal his glory to him on Mount Sinai (Exodus 33:18–22). On other occasions, to witness the glory of God meant to come under his judgment, as it did for the Hebrews who were grumbling about God's provisions when they fled from their captivity in Egypt (Exod. 16:7). Such experiences often generated fear and not comfort (Deuteronomy 5:25). In the New Testament, the glory (*doxa*) of God carries forward from the Old Testament the meaning of God's majesty and power. The New Testament writers witnessed this divine glory in the person of Jesus (Luke 9:32; 1 Corinthians 2:8; 2 Thessalonians 2:14). John reflected that understanding in our text when he connected this glory with Jesus (John 1:14).

APPLYING THE LESSON

You find yourself in a conversation with two people who are not Christian. As you witness to them, one challenges the belief that Jesus is unique and that one can know and experience God through any faith. How would you respond to this challenge? In what ways is Jesus unique?

QUESTIONS

1. If John were writing his Gospel to today's world, what categories would he use to communicate the story of Jesus?

2. What do the concepts of "life" and "light" teach us about Jesus?

3. What lessons can we learn from John the Baptist's response to Jesus?

4. Which aspect of Jesus do you tend to emphasize more—his humanity or his divinity? What are the dangers if we choose only his divinity? only his humanity?

5. What do you think John had in mind when he said that Jesus is "full of grace and truth"?

N O T E S

1. The Torah refers to the first five books of the Old Testament.

LESSON TWO

Jesus Revealing His Glory

MAIN IDEA

Jesus' turning the water into wine challenged Judaism's practices and revealed Jesus' identity as the Son of God.

QUESTION TO EXPLORE

So why *did* Jesus turn the water into wine?

STUDY AIM

To explain the significance of Jesus' turning the water into wine and state what it reveals to us about Jesus and what this means for our views and practices

QUICK READ

The miracle Jesus performed at the wedding feast in Cana was the first of the seven signs reflecting Jesus' unique power and distinct purpose reported in John's Gospel.

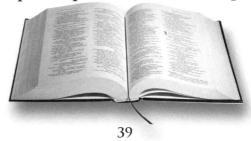

I have had my share of unusual happenings at weddings. In my first wedding, performed at the Belfalls Baptist Church in Central Texas, the wedding party, as well as the guests, all showed up at the church at the same time, ten minutes before the service. After I pronounced the couple husband and wife, the young man said to his new bride, "Let's gitty up and git on out of here!" And everybody left at the same time!

Over the years, various members of the wedding party, including the bride, have fainted or been rendered speechless by fear. One maid of honor threw up on the platform during the ceremony. Perhaps my strangest wedding was the one I performed in my office at the First Baptist Church in Pensacola, Florida. The bride was so bashful she would allow no one to be there except her and the groom. Even then, the weight of the moment overwhelmed her, and she passed out. The groom and I sat her on the couch, but she would not wake up. When she finally did wake up, she found she had a ring on her finger!

None of these experiences, however, compare to what happened at the wedding ceremony in Cana of Galilee. There Jesus saved the groom's family from social embarrassment by solving a dilemma relating to the wine. Of course, this story is more than just an unusual wedding story. It reveals some deep truths about the person and purpose of Jesus.

JOHN 2:1–11

1 On the third day a wedding took place at Cana in Galilee. Jesus' mother was there, 2 and Jesus and his disciples had also been invited to the wedding. 3 When the wine was gone, Jesus' mother said to him, "They have no more wine."

4 "Dear woman, why do you involve me?" Jesus replied. "My time has not yet come."

5 His mother said to the servants, "Do whatever he tells you."

6 Nearby stood six stone water jars, the kind used by the Jews for ceremonial washing, each holding from twenty to thirty gallons.

7 Jesus said to the servants, "Fill the jars with water"; so they filled them to the brim.

8 Then he told them, "Now draw some out and take it to the master of the banquet."

They did so, 9 and the master of the banquet tasted the water that had been turned into wine. He did not realize where it had come from, though the servants who had drawn the water knew. Then he called the bridegroom aside 10 and said, "Everyone brings out the choice wine first and then the cheaper wine after the guests have had too much to drink; but you have saved the best till now."

11 This, the first of his miraculous signs, Jesus performed at Cana in Galilee. He thus revealed his glory, and his disciples put their faith in him.

The Dilemma (2:1–3)

The author of the Fourth Gospel had introduced and identified Jesus in chapter 1 as the Word become flesh, full of grace and truth. John continued by building his portrait of Jesus around seven miracles that he called "signs" (John 2:11). The writer did not refer to the miracles as *wonders*, a word that describes their miraculous nature. Neither did he call them *acts of power*, a word that describes their explosive impact. Instead, he called them *signs*. A *sign* points beyond itself. The seven miracles in John's Gospel were not just magic tricks performed by Jesus to create wonder in the crowds of people following him, and neither were they simply random acts of power. Instead, they were signs pointing beyond themselves to the Miracle-worker.

So why did John present these seven signs? In part, he was motivated by his desire to reflect the glory manifest in this man called Jesus (2:12). But John's motive was not just to provide information. It was transformational. John wanted everyone to understand what the signs revealed about Jesus so that they would be transformed by their faith in him (20:31). The first of the signs, described in the text for today's lesson, took place at a wedding in Cana of Galilee.

We do not know whose wedding Jesus and his disciples attended. The celebration seemed to be moving along smoothly when something happened to cast a shadow over this joyous occasion. The host ran out of wine, an essential part of the wedding feast. A shortage of wine would have been a source of extreme embarrassment to the family of the groom. Apparently Mary felt responsible to solve the problem, and so she took it to Jesus, informing him that the supply of wine had been depleted. That she approached Jesus implied that she expected him to do something about the problem.

Why did Mary appeal to Jesus? Was it simply because he was her son and she expected him to assist her as any good son would? Or did she turn to Jesus because she remembered the unique prophecies made about her son, prophecies she had turned over in her mind during the thirty years since Jesus' extraordinary birth events? Did she simply expect his assistance, or did she expect a miracle? The text does not give a clear answer to these questions.

The Response (2:4–8)

John focused first on what Jesus said in response to his mother's request. Jesus' comment to his mother startles us at first glance. He referred to his mother as "woman" (2:4). This seems like a discourteous retort, but it was not. Using this term to refer to one's mother was natural at that time. It was a term of affection. On the surface, Jesus appeared to be refusing to help his mother, but he was not.

Jesus simply reminded her that the two of them operated on different levels. She perceived the problem through the lens of material need: the need for more wine. Jesus reflected on the problem through the lens of spiritual priorities: the need to establish God's kingdom on earth. Jesus wanted his mother to keep in mind the higher role to which he had been called. Mary did not sense any disrespect in Jesus' response. Neither did she believe he refused to help. She somehow communicated to Jesus that she clearly understood his point. Yet, she still expected him to help with this situation. That is why she instructed the servants to do whatever Jesus told them to do (2:5).

Realizing that his mother understood, Jesus acted to solve the dilemma (2:6–8). He pointed to six stone water jars and told the servants to fill them with water. John added two significant facts about these stone water jars. He explained that the Jews used water jars like these for ceremonial washing. With that comment, John implied a deeper meaning to the story. On the surface of the story, Jesus provided a better wine for the wedding guests, which was a material matter. At the deeper level, Jesus provided a better cleansing than that offered through the purification rites of the Jews, which was a spiritual matter.

John explained that each of these water jars held between 20 and 30 gallons of liquid. In this reference, John emphasized the generosity of Jesus' provision. The groom's family needed only a little more wine to satisfy their guests until the wedding celebration was over.

Instead of simply meeting the need, Jesus provided between 120 and 180 gallons of the very best wine available. He told the servants to fill completely the jars with water and then to draw some of the liquid out and take it to the master of the banquet. Again, the story moves on two levels. On the surface, Jesus met the need for more wine. At the deeper level, John highlighted Jesus' abundant spiritual provisions.

The Result (2:9–11)

John concluded the story by describing the result from the perspective of the master of the banquet and then from the perspective of the disciples. The master of the banquet responded with amazement and in so doing uncovered a common practice of the day (2:9–10). Apparently, the groom and his family commonly provided the very best wine at the beginning of the wedding celebration. Then, they provided a lower quality of wine for the last days of the celebration, believing that the guests' palates would be so dulled by this point that they could not tell any difference. However, when Jesus turned the water into "the best" wine, this groom's family appeared to reverse the common practice. They started with a lower quality of wine and then, at the end of the wedding celebration, they provided the highest quality wine. Again, John seems to be telling the story at two levels, the material level on the surface and then a deeper spiritual level. The groom's family provided a higher level of wine for their guests, even as Jesus would provide a higher level of spiritual nourishment for those who followed him.

The disciples responded with faith (2:11). This story is not primarily about Jesus' relationship to Mary, the expression of divine power, the relief of human discomfort, or the different quality of wines. This story declares the breaking of the new age of God into this age in which we live. This story affirms the inauguration of the kingdom of God in the midst of the kingdoms of earth. The kingdom of God is already at work among us. God has already begun to move us toward the new age he has in store for us. The eternal has already invaded the temporary, material world in which we live. The glory of God is already beginning to break through in the life of Jesus, and the disciples recognized this deeper level. John concluded, "and his disciples put their faith in him" (2:11). Why? They did not do this just because Jesus turned the water into wine. The disciples were beginning to realize that, because of what God was doing in Jesus Christ, everything was changed. A new day had dawned.

Implications and Actions

Jesus revealed three qualities of his life that clarify our understanding of who he is in this story. By his presence at the wedding, Jesus revealed his involvement in daily life. He was no recluse, avoiding anything that smacked of entertainment or amusement. On the contrary, from the beginning of his ministry, Jesus involved himself in life.

By providing wine, Jesus revealed his willingness to meet human needs. Spiritual needs were always important to Jesus, but his work was not limited to spiritual needs. Instead, from the beginning of his ministry, Jesus concerned himself with all levels of human need.

By the abundance of wine that he produced, Jesus revealed the overflowing abundance of his love. Not surprisingly, this Jesus of abundant provisions would later announce his purpose for coming in terms of abundance: "I have come that they may have life, and have it to the full" (John 10:10).

First-Century Weddings

Weddings in the first-century world were times of joyous celebration. Weddings were usually arranged in advance by families. One stage of the relationship, betrothal, resembled modern engagement but required legal action to dissolve. For some time the bride would remain in her father's house. Then, on the designated wedding night, the bride and her party would travel in a procession from her father's house to her future husband's house. As the procession made its way down the street, many of those standing along the way would join in the celebratory parade. When the procession arrived at the new home, the father of the bride would present his daughter to her husband. He would utter a solemn prayer, and the wedding party would ceremonially wash their hands. At that point, the celebration would begin. Sometimes these wedding festivals lasted a whole week.

CASE STUDY

A teacher in a Sunday School class claims that people usually present Jesus in terms that are too serious and devoid of any humor or joy. She suggests that we need to lighten up in our understanding of who Jesus is. One class member protests that we must not lighten up in our understanding of Jesus because the New Testament presents Jesus as a serious person. Based on the experience in our text, how would you respond?

QUESTIONS

1. Why do you think John chose this incident at the wedding feast at Cana as one of the *signs* to convince his readers that Jesus is the Son of God?

2. Why do you think Jesus responded to Mary the way he did when she asked for his help?

3. Why did Jesus provide such an abundance of wine?

4. In what way does this experience in today's text relate to your life today?

5. Which element of the experience most influenced the disciples to put their faith in Jesus?

LESSON THREE

Jesus' Authority as the Son of God

MAIN IDEA

Jesus' cleansing the temple signifies Jesus' authority as the Son of God over even the center of Jewish life, the temple, which his resurrection would verify.

QUESTION TO EXPLORE

How do we resist Jesus' authority over our own institutions, views, and actions?

STUDY AIM

To explain the significance of Jesus' cleansing the temple and state what it means for how we should respond to Jesus

QUICK READ

When Jesus saw the merchandising of cattle and exchange of currency in the temple, he reacted passionately and cleared the temple of the money changers and merchants.

Several months before I retired as pastor of First Baptist Church of Richardson, Texas, a young woman who was a member of the church came to see me. Her father was a pastor. At the last church he served, he was unjustly criticized and constantly opposed until finally the church voted to remove him as its pastor. I asked her how she felt about what had happened to her father. She told me she was bitter at first but that she had worked through it. She then made this statement about her brother, who handled the dismissal differently: "He won't get anywhere near a church. He still believes in God. He just doesn't believe in the church."

Her brother's belief about the church reflects the view of the spiritual life of many in the twenty-first century. While we are witnessing a renewed interest in spirituality in America, many people do not turn to the church to find their spiritual answers. Instead, they search for spiritual experiences outside the church. These people desire to be spiritual, but they have written off the church. For them, the church seems to be more *in* their way to God than *on* the way to God.

Jesus expressed a discontent with established religion in his visit to the temple as described in today's text. Solomon had built the magnificent structure in Jerusalem known as the temple. The returning exiles had rebuilt it after it was destroyed by Nebuchadnezzar. Later still, Herod enlarged it even more. The prophet Isaiah declared the purpose of the temple when he announced these words from God: "My house will be called a house of prayer for all the nations" (Isaiah 56:7). However, Jesus discovered that instead of encouraging people to pray, the religious practices in the temple of his day actually prevented people from praying. Asserting his authority, he reacted to correct the perversion.

JOHN 2:13–22

13 When it was almost time for the Jewish Passover, Jesus went up to Jerusalem. **14** In the temple courts he found men selling cattle, sheep and doves, and others sitting at tables exchanging money. **15** So he made a whip out of cords, and drove all from the temple area, both sheep and cattle; he scattered the coins of the money changers and overturned their tables. **16** To those who sold doves he said, "Get these out of here! How dare you turn my Father's house into a market!"

17 His disciples remembered that it is written: "Zeal for your house will consume me."

18 Then the Jews demanded of him, "What miraculous sign can you show us to prove your authority to do all this?"

19 Jesus answered them, "Destroy this temple, and I will raise it again in three days."

20 The Jews replied, "It has taken forty-six years to build this temple, and you are going to raise it in three days?"

²¹ But the temple he had spoken of was his body. ²² After he was raised from the dead, his disciples recalled what he had said. Then they believed the Scripture and the words that Jesus had spoken.

What Jesus Saw (2:13–14)

Jesus traveled to Jerusalem with his disciples to celebrate the Passover. When he arrived in Jerusalem, he went to the temple. What he saw when he came to the Court of the Gentiles, the one place in the temple where the Gentiles could come to pray, appalled him. He saw "men selling cattle, sheep and doves" (John 2:14). When worshipers came to the temple, they would sacrifice an animal such as a dove or a lamb. For convenience, the priests allowed merchants to set up booths in the Court of the Gentiles to provide these animals. However, greedy merchants soon perverted the system by charging exorbitant prices for the animals. Worshipers did not have to buy these animals from the merchants. They could instead bring an animal for sacrifice with them. However, the priests had to approve these animals. To support the merchants, the priests would refuse to approve most of the animals worshipers brought in from the outside, thus forcing the worshipers to buy one of the animals provided by the merchants. While enriching the merchants, this arrangement penalized the worshipers. Further, this collection of animals in the temple filled the Court of the Gentiles with the sounds and smells of a barnyard, creating a context of confusion rather than a context conducive to worship.

Jesus saw "others sitting at tables exchanging money" (2:14). Who were these money changers? Remember that many of the worshipers came from countries far away, bringing with them Greek, Roman, and Egyptian currencies. However, foreign money could not be used in the temple. Worshipers could use only Jewish coins to pay the temple tax and to fulfill the various rites of purification. Therefore, the temple featured a series of money changers, also set up in the Court of the Gentiles, to exchange this foreign currency with Jewish coins. Naturally, the money changers charged a fee for the favor. Over time, the fees increased, and the money changers profited from their excessive charges. This procedure again fleeced the pilgrims who came to the temple to worship God. All of this took place with the support and approval of the priests. That is what Jesus saw as he entered the temple that day. He saw the temple area being desecrated, the faithful pilgrims being fleeced, and the merchants and religious leaders getting rich.

What Jesus Did (2:15–17)

Jesus responded with deliberate action. Each of the four accounts of Jesus' experience in the temple provides a slightly different perspective (see Matthew 21:12–13; Mark 11:15–17; Luke 19:45–46), but John's account includes some unique elements. For example, only the Gospel of John tells us Jesus made a whip out of cords (John 2:15). Perhaps Jesus constructed the whip out of some branches that provided bedding for the larger animals. The Greek word suggests the use of such branches.

Only the Gospel of John reveals that Jesus drove all these merchants out of the temple, including their sheep and cattle (2:15). Only John mentions the more expensive animals such as cattle and sheep. The other accounts in the Synoptic Gospels refer to the pigeons and doves, the sin offering presented by the poor (Leviticus 5:7). Perhaps John wanted his readers to believe that Jesus treated the owners of the cattle and sheep more harshly than those who owned the doves, perhaps because doves were the animals of sacrifice used by the poor. More likely, we can explain the distinction between Jesus' responses to the two groups in a more practical way. It is easy to see how Jesus could drive the cattle and sheep out. On the other hand, the doves, in their cages, had to be carried out. If Jesus released the birds from their cages, they would fly away. However we interpret John's references to sheep and cattle and his description of exactly what Jesus did, John's point is nevertheless clear. These merchants who were fleecing the worshipers for their own personal gain transformed the temple from a place of worship into a merchant shop, and Jesus would not allow them to continue.

Jesus also turned over the tables on which the money changers carried out their work and scattered their coins throughout the Court of the Gentiles. Notice the contrast between "my Father's house" (what the temple should be) and "a market" (what the temple had become). So Jesus ran the money changers out because he would not allow God's house of prayer to be turned into a house of merchandise.

At this point, John inserted a comment concerning the disciples (John 2:17). Jesus' action evoked in the minds of the disciples a passage from Psalm 69 that they had probably memorized as children. The early Christians understood this psalm that described the suffering and misunderstanding of David to be a prediction of the suffering the Messiah would experience. Since they considered Jesus to be the Messiah, they applied this passage to Jesus. Recalling Psalm 69:9 and relating it to the action of Jesus in the temple did not console the disciples but disturbed them, for they realized that Jesus' actions that day in the temple would provoke retaliation from the religious leaders. As a result, Jesus would experience the same kind of suffering David described in Psalm 69.

What Jesus Said (2:18–22)

The religious leaders, of course, would not leave Jesus' actions unchallenged. Jesus might intimidate the money changers and animal-keepers, but the religious leaders were not intimidated so easily. Instead of ignoring Jesus' outburst, they confronted him with a demand. They wanted to know by what authority he disturbed the ebb and flow of the activities in the temple (2:18). In his answer, using metaphorical language, Jesus pointed to the resurrection. He told his critics that if they destroyed "this temple" he would raise it again in three days (2:18). Jesus was actually talking about his body as the temple. *Kill this body*, Jesus declared, *and three days later I will arise from the dead as the victorious, resurrected Lord.* The religious leaders took Jesus' statement literally. They thought he was speaking of the temple in Jerusalem. That is why they responded with incredulity. Such a structure as the temple would take decades to rebuild. In fact, the work of restoring the temple had been going on since 19 B.C. The leaders understood Jesus to be claiming that he was able to accomplish that feat in three days.

Even the disciples did not understand Jesus at this point. Perhaps the thought that Jesus could be put to death was too terrible for them to contemplate. The thought of someone coming back from the grave just did not sync with their understanding. Only after the resurrection did the disciples realize the point of Jesus' metaphor, that he was talking about the destruction of his physical body and his resurrection three days later. At that point, Psalm 16:10 might have come to mind as the psalmist declared: "Because you will not abandon me to the grave, nor will you let your Holy One see decay" (Psalm 16:10).

Applying the Lesson to Life

What is the church? Some say it is a religious country club, a gathering of homogenous people of common interests with special rules for entry and sacred rituals to follow. Others see it as a relic of the past, an anachronism in our modern world of science and technology that simply needs to be discarded. Still others suggest the church is a museum of ancient history, led by pastors who serve as curators of the museums and guardians of the ancient manuscripts.

What is the church? According to the story in our text, the church is a group of people who create an environment that is conducive to worship and inviting to those who want to worship. How do our churches fit that two-fold profile of the church—an environment that is conducive to worship and inviting? If Jesus were to attend our churches this week, what would he see?

THE TEMPLE

The temple in Jesus' day was known as Herod's temple, because he began rebuilding it in 19 B.C. The rebuilt temple featured a series of porches inside a walled-off area. The south porch was known as the Royal Porch. Solomon's Porch extended along the east side of the temple. In the center of the temple area, slightly raised above the outer court, was the inner area of the temple, which included the Court of the Women, the Court of Israel, and the inner sanctuary. A wall with a limited number of entrances surrounded this inner court. Notices in Greek and Latin posted at these entrances warned Gentiles not to enter this inner area. The area between the outer wall and this inner area was known as the Court of the Gentiles. Gentiles who desired to worship the God of Israel and learn more about him could come only into this outer area. The tables of the money changers and the stalls containing the animals mentioned in John 2:1–11 were located in this area.

How Your Church Appears

As you attend church this Sunday, consider how your church might appear to a first-time guest.

- Notice the building itself and how it makes you feel.
- Be sensitive to how the greeters welcome you.
- Note the actions and words spoken in your Bible study class.
- Pay attention to everything that is said and done in the worship service.
- When you get home, make a list of things you can do to make your church more conducive to worship and more inviting to guests.
- Share your list with your class and other leaders in your church.

QUESTIONS

1. What parallels do you see between the practices in the temple described in today's text and the practices of churches today?

2. Do the actions of your church on Sunday morning and your practices in worship create a context of confusion or do they create a context that is conducive to worship?

3. Have you observed any practices of your church that would make guests feel uncomfortable?

4. If you knew Jesus was going to attend your church next Sunday, what changes would you make?

LESSON FOUR

The Smartest, Most Religious Person in the Room

MAIN IDEA

Jesus' conversation with Nicodemus reveals that real life comes from being "born from above" through belief in Jesus as God's Son.

QUESTION TO EXPLORE

What is the source of real life?

STUDY AIM

To explain the meaning of Jesus' conversation with Nicodemus and consider how I need to respond

QUICK READ

Jesus described the concept of a new birth and eternal life to Nicodemus, a Pharisee and a ruler of the Jews. Nicodemus needed a personal experience with God to be the person God intended him to be.

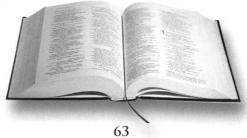

People, although diverse, have much in common. Down-and-out people need Jesus Christ. So do people with all the opportunities, education, and gadgets of an affluent, materialistic world. *Up-and-in* can be just as lost as *down-and-out*. A *smart-as-a-whip* person can be as much in need as one who is *dumb-as-a-rock*. Nicodemus represented the finest of Jewish religion and society.

JOHN 3:1–16

1 Now there was a man of the Pharisees named Nicodemus, a member of the Jewish ruling council. **2** He came to Jesus at night and said, "Rabbi, we know you are a teacher who has come from God. For no one could perform the miraculous signs you are doing if God were not with him."

3 In reply Jesus declared, "I tell you the truth, no one can see the kingdom of God unless he is born again."

4 "How can a man be born when he is old?" Nicodemus asked. "Surely he cannot enter a second time into his mother's womb to be born!"

5 Jesus answered, "I tell you the truth, no one can enter the kingdom of God unless he is born of water and the Spirit. **6** Flesh gives birth to flesh, but the Spirit gives birth to spirit. **7** You should not be surprised at my saying, 'You must be born again.' **8** The wind blows wherever it pleases. You hear its sound, but you cannot tell where it comes from or where it is going. So it is with everyone born of the Spirit."

9 "How can this be?" Nicodemus asked.

10 "You are Israel's teacher," said Jesus, "and do you not understand these things? **11** I tell you the truth, we speak of what we know, and we testify to what we have seen, but still you people do not accept our testimony. **12** I have spoken to you of earthly things and you do not believe; how then will you believe if I speak of heavenly things? **13** No one has ever gone into heaven except the one who came from heaven—the Son of Man. **14** Just as Moses lifted up the snake in the desert, so the Son of Man must be lifted up, **15** that everyone who believes in him may have eternal life.

16 "For God so loved the world that he gave his one and only Son, that whoever believes in him shall not perish but have eternal life.

Wrong Ways to Get to God (3:1–2)

Nicodemus seemed to have it all going for him. He was a distinguished Pharisee and a member of the Sanhedrin, the ruling authority in Jerusalem. He was a prominent teacher. He appears in John's Gospel two more times: once when defending Jesus before some of his more zealous brethren (John 7:45–52) and later when he went with Joseph of Arimathea to take Jesus' body off the cross to bury it (19:38–42). Nicodemus may have even become a disciple himself. His story has become a familiar and important part of God's message to us.

That "he came to Jesus by night" (3:2) may not suggest a secretive intent. Perhaps a late night conversation was the only time when Nicodemus could have a long visit with Jesus. His coming could have been for personal reasons, but he also could have represented the groups with which he was involved in Judaism. Nicodemus opened the conversation by saying, "we know you are a teacher who has come from God" (3:2). Later Jesus said "You must be born again" (3:7). "You" translates a plural form of the pronoun. Nicodemus's coming may have addressed both personal needs and those from his religious community.

Nicodemus's first words link today's text to John 2:23–25. Nicodemus was a prime example of the people mentioned there who turned to Jesus because of his miracles and signs. They recognized that God was with Jesus, but the Scripture says, "Jesus would not entrust himself to them" (2:24). Jesus knew theirs was a *cut-flower* adoration and was not rooted in life-changing belief. Nicodemus was correct in saying that Jesus was a teacher come from God, but Jesus led Nicodemus to see that Jesus was more than that.

Nicodemus represented the finest of Jewish tradition, but that tradition was lacking. Although it afforded the background for Jesus' ministry and the emergence of the Christian church, it was flawed (see Hebrews 8:6–7; Matthew 23). The thrust of Judaism was to get right with

God by keeping the law and scrupulously following religious rituals. To Nicodemus, Jesus was an interesting option, but Nicodemus was still trying to get right with God the wrong way.

Jesus Guides Nicodemus (3:2–15)

The conversation between Jesus and Nicodemus has three movements. We saw some of the first movement in John 3:2. Nicodemus began politely and positively, but Jesus abruptly turned the conversation to a deeper level: "no one can see the kingdom of God unless he is born again." That must have startled Nicodemus, for he was a son of Abraham. By physical birth he was both a Jew and one of God's children.

Jesus said Nicodemus needed to be "born again." Jews referred to the conversion of Gentiles to Judaism as a "new birth," but they never would have said that about themselves. Jesus was telling a respected leader of Judaism that he needed to be born again. To be in God's kingdom, more was needed than just being a Jewish male. Nicodemus needed a new beginning. Interestingly, the Greek word translated "born again" is also translated *born from above*. Both translations are appropriate.

Being "born again" allows a person to experience the "kingdom of God." In John 3:3, Jesus said that unless you have been born again, you cannot "see" the kingdom of

God. Some things may not make sense from the outside, but when you are in the kingdom, you see much better. Jesus added that without the new birth you cannot "enter" the kingdom of God (John 3:5). Some define "kingdom of God" as a king and his rule in the universe. We see and enter the kingdom through a new birth that aligns our lives and loyalty to the king of the kingdom. We do not build the kingdom, but we can pray for it to be extended and recognized on earth as it is in heaven (Matthew 6:10).

The second part of the conversation is in John 3:4–8. When Jesus introduced the idea of the new birth, Nicodemus raised the *how* question. Mary asked the same thing when told about her pregnancy: "how can this be?" (Luke 1:34). Nicodemus followed up his question by commenting on the impossibility of reentering his mother's womb. Jesus' response was to point to several words of analogy and explanation: water, Spirit, flesh, wind, earthly things, and heavenly things. Sorting these out may lead us to ask again with Nicodemus, "how . . . ?"

The primary contrast is between physical birth and spiritual birth. Water may refer to physical birth and spirit to spiritual birth although some argue for a baptismal interpretation.

The wind is another analogy to the Spirit and provides an interesting paradox to the analogy of being "born again." When does "born again" take place? Jesus compared it to the wind. You may not know the time, date, and place the wind began, but you do know you are in the breeze. People who have been "born again" are "born of the Spirit," and the old ways of getting to God through ritual and keeping the law are replaced by the Spirit's causing a new beginning in one's life. Later in today's text, believing will be introduced as our cooperative response to what God's Spirit is doing. Paul reaffirmed that in Ephesians 2:8, when he noted we are saved by grace through faith.

A learned leader such as Nicodemus would have known the story of Ezekiel and the valley of dry bones. In Ezekiel 37:1–14, Israel was compared to a valley of dry bones, but the wind (God's Spirit) brought back to life a spiritually dead Israel. Jesus was teaching that God's Spirit is still in the business of bringing new life. Nicodemus, as well as all the groups he represented, needed this fresh movement of the Spirit.

The third movement of conversation is John 3:9–15. Having heard Jesus' explanation, Nicodemus raised the question: "How can this be"? Jesus had spoken in earthly analogies, but Nicodemus did not catch on. Perhaps Nicodemus's filter was not allowing the new application of grace and spirit to run, for he still thought in terms of law and ritual. Nicodemus could go no further at this point, but as we noted earlier, he was present and publicly connected to Jesus at Jesus' death (19:38–42).

Jesus closed the conversation by telling Nicodemus that he, the Son of Man, had come from heaven. Jesus anticipated his crucifixion with his reference to Moses in the wilderness (Numbers 21:4–9). Again, Jesus used an earthly experience to point to a profound spiritual truth. As Moses had lifted a bronzed serpent that provided healing for Hebrews in the desert, Jesus would be lifted up on a cross that would provide eternal life to all who believed.

For God So Loved the World (3:16)

John followed up the conversation between Nicodemus and Jesus with what Martin Luther called "The Little Bible." Many have suggested that if we suddenly lost the entire Bible and had only John 3:16, we would have enough. Apparently, God does not think so, but that idea indicates the fullness and richness that Christians find in John 3:16.

God's nature is one of love. As one reads through the writings of John, including the Letters of John, it is abundantly clear that love is a dominant quality of God and that it should also permeate the life of every believer. The love of John 3:16 is an *agape* love, a godly kind of love that is willing to sacrifice for the good of another. The "world" refers to every person, to those who are hostile to God. God does not discriminate among people.

In the conversation with Nicodemus, Jesus brought up the kingdom of God and being born again by the Spirit. In John 3:15, "eternal life" was introduced along with the importance of believing. Since only God and his kingdom are eternal, eternal life is the presence of God in our lives now and the continuing experience with God after death in heaven. God wants all people to enjoy that. As Peter wrote, the Lord is patient, "not wanting anyone to perish" (2 Peter 3:9).

Nicodemus had a hard time understanding why he needed a new birth and how it was accomplished. Others may be in his shoes. But as John 3:16 indicates, people will perish if they do not believe. Although many good and sincere people are not followers of Christ, how much better and greater could they be if they were connected to the ultimate power and presence of this universe?

Implications and Actions

You may be reading this lesson because someone helped you understand who Jesus was and helped you to commit your life to him. You may have gone through extensive searching, perhaps with questions similar to those of Nicodemus. Or you may have been raised to trust Jesus from your earliest memories, and a commitment to Jesus was a natural progression of your experiences in your family and church.

When a person becomes a Christian, it is a work of God, but a work in which God continues to use us in the process. If you have not been "born again," I pray that you will submit your life and will to Jesus today and receive him as your Lord and Savior. But, if you have already made that decision, do not keep it to yourself. Let the Lord use your life and lips to point people to Jesus.

People like Nicodemus abound. People without hope for eternity surround us. Someone has said that the church exists for those who are not in it. If that be so, what will we do so others can experience the blessings of eternal life?

THE WORDS OF JESUS

In some translations, the words of Jesus are printed in red. Although we may attach special significance to these words, sometimes it is hard to know when Jesus' words start or end. For example, some scholars see Jesus' conversation with Nicodemus ending with verse 10. The plural pronouns that follow (*you* and *our*) may indicate that Jesus or John used some of the Nicodemus material to make broader application concerning the leaders and laity of Israel. Some see Jesus' comments going through John 3:15, thinking that the pronouns are editorial devices that do not invalidate the personal interaction with Nicodemus. Others break the comments at verse 12 or verse 21. While I prefer 3:15 and such a study may be interesting, it does not change the interpretation of the passage.

FOR GOD SO LOVED THE WORLD

What if Nicodemus would have visited Jesus at a later time to talk about "God so loved the world" and Jesus said, *I don't have time now but why don't you come back just before I go to heaven?* Then Nicodemus complied and arrived just in time to hear Jesus say, "Be my witnesses in Jerusalem, and in all Judea and Samaria, and to the ends of the earth" (Acts 1:8). Suppose you were Nicodemus, how would you apply that comment to the twenty-first century? What plan would you draw up to guide your church into a "for God so loved the world" mentality?

QUESTIONS

1. If you could have a long talk with your pastor about spiritual matters, what would you like to talk about?

2. What would you say if someone asked you, *How do you become a Christian?*

3. What will you do for those people you know who are not Christians or appear to have no meaningful relationship with Jesus Christ or a church?

4. What can your class do to reach people who are not involved in Bible study and/or church?

5. Since the church is the extension of the reality and nature of God into the world, how can your church more effectively share the love of God with those who live nearby?

LESSON FIVE

The Source of Fulfillment

MAIN IDEA

Jesus' conversation with the Samaritan woman shows that "living water" is available to all but only from Jesus.

QUESTIONS TO EXPLORE

Where are you seeking fulfillment in life? What can you do to help others find it?

STUDY AIM

To explain the meaning of Jesus' conversation with the Samaritan woman and consider how I need to respond myself and in my relationships with others

QUICK READ

Jesus challenged cultural norms of his day by engaging a woman from Samaria in conversation at a well where he sat to rest. He helped the woman to see beyond her current situation and struggles and ultimately to recognize him as the Christ.

While I was growing up, my family occasionally visited my grandparents who lived near the mountains of Northeast Georgia. Of the many things I could do there, I especially enjoyed the well. Soon after arriving, I would go to the well, throw the bucket on the rope into the well, draw the bucket up slowly, and then take the dipper and sip the cool, clear water.

Today's Scripture focuses on a woman who met an unusual man at a well. In the culture in which they lived, the male stranger and the woman would not normally have spoken to each other, let alone have a lengthy and intimate conversation. The encounter changed her life.

JOHN 4:4–30, 39–42

4 Now he had to go through Samaria. **5** So he came to a town in Samaria called Sychar, near the plot of ground Jacob had given to his son Joseph. **6** Jacob's well was there, and Jesus, tired as he was from the journey, sat down by the well. It was about the sixth hour.

7 When a Samaritan woman came to draw water, Jesus said to her, "Will you give me a drink?" **8** (His disciples had gone into the town to buy food.)

9 The Samaritan woman said to him, "You are a Jew and I am a Samaritan woman. How can you ask me for a drink?" (For Jews do not associate with Samaritans.)

10 Jesus answered her, "If you knew the gift of God and who it is that asks you for a drink, you would have asked him and he would have given you living water."

11 "Sir," the woman said, "you have nothing to draw with and the well is deep. Where can you get this living water? **12** Are you greater than our father Jacob, who gave us the well and drank from it himself, as did also his sons and his flocks and herds?"

13 Jesus answered, "Everyone who drinks this water will be thirsty again, **14** but whoever drinks the water I give him will never thirst. Indeed, the water I give him will become in him a spring of water welling up to eternal life."

15 The woman said to him, "Sir, give me this water so that I won't get thirsty and have to keep coming here to draw water."

16 He told her, "Go, call your husband and come back."

17 "I have no husband," she replied.

Jesus said to her, "You are right when you say you have no husband. **18** The fact is, you have had five husbands, and the man you now have is not your husband. What you have just said is quite true."

19 "Sir," the woman said, "I can see that you are a prophet. **20** Our fathers worshiped on this mountain, but you Jews claim that the place where we must worship is in Jerusalem."

21 Jesus declared, "Believe me, woman, a time is coming when you will worship the Father neither on this mountain nor in Jerusalem. **22** You Samaritans worship what you do not know; we worship what we do know, for salvation is from the Jews. **23** Yet a time is coming and has now come when the true worshipers will worship the Father in spirit and truth, for they are the kind of worshipers the Father seeks. **24** God is spirit, and his worshipers must worship in spirit and in truth."

25 The woman said, "I know that Messiah" (called Christ) "is coming. When he comes, he will explain everything to us."

26 Then Jesus declared, "I who speak to you am he."

27 Just then his disciples returned and were surprised to find him talking with a woman. But no one asked, "What do you want?" or "Why are you talking with her?"

28 Then, leaving her water jar, the woman went back to the town and said to the people, **29** "Come, see a man who told me everything I ever did. Could this be the Christ?" **30** They came out of the town and made their way toward him.

• • • • • • • • • • • • • • • • • • • •

39 Many of the Samaritans from that town believed in him because of the woman's testimony, "He told me everything I ever did." **40** So when the Samaritans came to him, they urged him to stay with them, and he stayed two days. **41** And because of his words many more became believers.

42 They said to the woman, "We no longer believe just because of what you said; now we have heard for ourselves, and we know that this man really is the Savior of the world."

A Teachable Moment in Samaria (4:4–9)

Just before his ascension, Jesus commissioned his disciples to witness concerning him in Jerusalem, Judea, Samaria, and to the ends of the earth (Acts 1:6–8). Previous chapters in John's Gospel have found Jesus in Jerusalem (John 2:13–31) and Judea (3:22–36). This lesson's Scripture passage places him in Samaria

Traveling through Samaria was the most direct way between Judea and Galilee. That, however, was not the normal travel pattern for a Jew, for Jews despised Samaritans. The feeling was mutual. Jesus' encounter with this woman in Samaria became a teachable moment for the Samaritans he met as well as his disciples.

Jesus stopped at Sychar, the traditional site of Jacob's well, around noon. Jesus was tired, and he and the disciples were hungry. While the disciples were in the village buying food, a Samaritan woman showed up.

Women usually went to the well early or late in the day, when the temperature was cooler, but this woman came to the well at noon. Jesus asked her for a drink. Such a request was not proper conduct for their culture for two reasons: men and women did not carry on conversations in public, and Jews and Samaritans did not get along. Jesus crossed the barriers of race, religion, and gender. People still erect these barriers today.

The Promise of Living Water (4:10–18)

The Samaritan woman is introduced in the Gospel of John in the chapter after the experience with Nicodemus. These two people illustrate Jesus' interest in and love for everyone. One was an unnamed woman from Samaria, with little or no status. The other was a named Jewish male, an elite and orthodox religious teacher who was well known and respected in his city. In the conclusion to their stories, one affirmed Jesus as the Christ, and the other was thinking about it. The contrast between the two is striking, but they reveal that all people need a vital relationship with Jesus Christ, regardless of heredity or social distinction.

The conversation with the Samaritan woman proceeded in a manner similar to the conversation Jesus had with Nicodemus. The use of two levels of conversation—the contrast between the physical and the spiritual, the earthly and the heavenly—are apparent. The conversation began with a simple request from Jesus, "Will you give me a drink?" It moved quickly to living water and the satisfaction of a spiritual thirst that only comes from God.

Jesus turned around the woman's response to his request for a drink by telling the woman that if she knew who he really was, she would ask him and he would provide "living water" (4:10). She looked at him, wondering how he could provide water for her when he did not have a bucket. She opened the door for Jesus to move more deeply. He did not get into discussions about greatness. Instead, perhaps pointing to the water she gave him, Jesus told her that the need for normal water would reoccur, but that he could provide water for her that would lead to eternal life.

As he did with Nicodemus, Jesus spoke with the woman about "eternal life." The woman apparently did not get the connection between eternal life and living water. She asked Jesus where she could get that kind of water so she would not need to draw water from the well anymore. To that, Jesus told her to get her husband and return to him.

The woman replied that she had no husband. Jesus affirmed the truthfulness of her answer, but he countered that she had had five marriages and that she was not married to her current live-in. She thirsted for something deeper and better. Jesus stated the facts of her relationships, but there is no record that he passed judgment on her. Her response indicated she was growing uncomfortable but perhaps catching on. She assumed Jesus was a prophet, for he saw deeply into her life and spoke of a new day coming.

True Worship (4:19–27)

The woman attempted to change the subject of the conversation. Samaritans thought it suitable to worship on Mount Gerizim, although their temple had been destroyed a century earlier. Jews thought Jerusalem was the place for sacred feasts, celebrations, and true worship. Each group stubbornly persisted in following their exclusive claims about God. The woman knew this history, but Jesus took her beyond her traditional understanding which was shaped by "our fathers [who] worshiped on this mountain." Jesus told her of a new day that was coming.

Jesus spoke of worshiping God in spirit and in truth (4:24). True worship is based on a true God, but it is not limited to a particular place. Although God used Israel as his vehicle to get his message to the world, God did not limit himself to Israel or to the Jews. Jesus has revealed the true Father (1:18), and those who worship God do so "in spirit" because God is spirit, not limited by human distinctions or barriers. True worship is inclusive of all who call on the name of Jesus. Jesus is the way to life (14:6).

The woman's beliefs were moving in the right direction. She first had seemed to misunderstand and even to jest about a bucket and *magic* water. Probing more deeply, Jesus had asked her to bring her husband. She denied she had a husband. Jesus told her what he knew about that. She had tried to avoid her need by debating about worship, but Jesus rejected that argument by injecting a deeper understanding of worship. Through it all, she was moving closer to genuine faith. Then she brought up the issue of the Messiah and how the Messiah would make everything clear. Jesus said, "I who speak to you am he."

At this point, the disciples returned from town, where they had gone to buy food. They saw Jesus talking to the Samaritan woman. That surprised them, but they made no comment to her or to Jesus. Could they have been slow catching on as well? At that point, Jesus had a teachable moment, indicating that his "food" was to do God's will and accomplish God's purpose in his life. The disciples struggled with what he meant (4:31–38).

The Samaritans Understand Who Jesus Is (4:28–30, 39–42)

Nicodemus said that Jesus was a teacher come from God (3:2). Good teachers are delighted when their students understand. Now a Samaritan woman was absorbed in Jesus' teaching. She was experiencing living water. Leaving her water jar, she went back home, telling her friends about Jesus and inviting them to "come, see." She posed the question, "Could this be the Christ?" The hope for a Messiah burned bright in the Samaritans' hearts as well as in the Jews. At her invitation, the Samaritans went out to see Jesus.

The principle that believers tell non-believers is still true today. When we have experienced something with God, it is too good to hold to ourselves. We saw this earlier in the Gospel of John, where John the Baptist, Andrew, Peter, and Philip passed on the word about Jesus to someone else

(1:35–50). The Scripture says that the Samaritans believed in Jesus because of the woman's testimony (4:40). Their further response was to invite Jesus to stay with them. He, along with his disciples, stayed two additional days with them.

The Samaritans first believed because of the testimony of the woman, but "because of his [Jesus'] words, many more became believers." Gratefully, these Samaritans acknowledged their indebtedness to the woman for her witness, but with Jesus present, they were able to hear firsthand about who he was and how he could change their lives. The Samaritans came to know Jesus for who he really was, the Savior of the world. John's prologue was confirmed: "to all who received him, to those who believed in his name, he gave the right to become children of God" (1:12–13). These Samaritans, excluded from interactions with Jews and thought to be separated from God because of their religion, had found new life in Christ. Neither Jerusalem's mountain nor Samaria's mountain can define or confine God. We thank God that Jesus "had to go through Samaria" (4:4).

Taking It Personally

How do we personalize today's Scripture? Christians embrace the general realities of the Great Commandment and the Great Commission, but do we embrace the call of

God to involvement with *all* people in salvation and service? Who are the Samaritans in your neighborhood? Are you willing to listen and spend time with them? Are you involved in changing structures that discriminate against people and in personally ministering to the world at your doorstep?

Jesus intentionally went to Samaria. He crossed the cultural barriers that kept most Jewish men from having conversation with a Samaritan woman, regardless of her reputation. Jesus' example and the full teaching of the New Testament challenge us to do a more effective job of loving people as God loves them, while sharing the good news of "the Savior of the world" to all people.

Nicodemus needed to be born again. The Samaritan woman needed living water. The figures of speech are different, but the reality is essentially the same. Both needed to accept Jesus for who he was and commit their lives to following him. Through their belief in Jesus, they could experience eternal life, a life filled with meaning and purpose in this life and forever. Jesus could fulfill their deepest needs.

SAMARIA

In biblical times, Samaria was the geographic center of Palestine, lying between Galilee and Judea. The nation divided into two kingdoms after King Solomon's death.

Throughout the history of divided Israel, Samaria and Judea were rivals. After the fall of Samaria (the Northern Kingdom) to Assyria in 722 B.C, many people were deported, and many people from other lands were brought to Samaria. With intermarriage to the foreigners, the Jewishness of the area was, in the minds of those from Judea, tainted. The Samaritans became objects of animosity to traditional Jews in Jerusalem.

By the time of Jesus, this animosity was mutual and long-standing. Jesus, though, chose to go through Samaria. In his marching orders to the church, he included Samaria (Acts 1:6–8). In Acts, one of the first missions outside Jerusalem and Judea was in Samaria (see Acts 8). Although Jesus began his earthly life as a baby of Jewish parentage, his mission was universal. "For God so loved the world" included Samaria (John 3:16).

SAMARITAN WATCH

Who are the Samaritans today? Today Samaritans may be people who often seem to be ignored or shunned, even by we who consider ourselves Christians. Identify Samaritans near you—the people who are left out, looked down on, or judged for one reason or another, perhaps because of their life choices but perhaps because of situations over which they have no control. Then (1) cross the cultural line; (2) build a relationship with one of these Samaritans; (3) love them like Jesus loves them; and (4) through the constancy of your life, help them to see the One who is "the Savior of the world" (John 4:42).

THE SAMARITAN WOMAN

In Jesus' dealings with the Samaritan woman, he revealed that he had a higher view of women than did others in his society. Jesus' relationship to the Samaritan woman, to Mary and Martha (Luke 10:38–42), to the adulterous woman (John 8:2–11), and to other women in his life (Luke 7:36—8:3) opened the doors for women to participate fully in God's mission through the church. Consider these Scriptures concerning the freedom of women to serve out their calling: Acts 2:17–18; Acts 21:8–9; Romans 16:1–15; Galatians 3:28.

QUESTIONS

1. How does God affect your life at the point of your desires and needs?

2. How can your class increase the circle of its impact in the world by reaching out to *Samaritans*, people who some may look down on?

3. The woman left her water jar to tell others about Jesus. What are you willing to leave or give up so others can know about Jesus?

4. Water is carried in buckets. If your life were the bucket and it was filled with living water, who needs to feel the splashes of that water in their lives?

FOCAL TEXT

John 4:46–54

BACKGROUND

John 4:43–54

LESSON SIX

Signs-Faith *or True Faith?*

MAIN IDEA

Jesus' healing of the royal official's son showed Jesus' power and led the official to express true faith.

QUESTION TO EXPLORE

Is your faith based on an expectation of miraculous acts from Jesus, or is it true commitment of life to Jesus based on who Jesus is?

STUDY AIM

To explain the significance of Jesus' healing the royal official's son and analyze whether my faith means true commitment of life to Jesus

QUICK READ

Jesus questioned the sincerity of those who followed him only because he performed miracles. He recognized real faith in a father who begged him to heal his son, and he healed the boy.

Several years ago, I was driving from Atlanta, Georgia, toward Nashville, Tennessee, and decided to take a short-cut. We did not have a GPS; I was just following a map. At first, the road was well-maintained, but the turns became numerous, and the quality of the road was not good. After driving about ten miles, I came to a sign that read, "Road Ends in 2 Miles." I thought, *Surely not.* After a short drive, there was a second sign: "This Is Not a Through Road." By the condition of the road, I knew the signs must be right. I turned back.

We all have made some mistakes when traveling, but most are correctable. We may take a wrong turn, but we arrive safely. Some roads are crooked, some are bumpy, and some are dead-ends.

In life, we often take wrong turns and sometimes have to pay for them. We follow roads that lead to nowhere. Although we may think we know where we are going, we find that our destination is not what we thought it would be.

God knew the world was headed in the wrong direction. He did all kinds of things to turn it around. Finally, God came uniquely in Jesus: "the Word became flesh and made his dwelling among us" (John 1:14). John chose only a few events in Jesus' life to which to give detailed attention. Some of these were "signs," written so people would believe in Jesus and, through believing, have new life in him. Today's text records an encounter between Jesus and a royal official whose son was gravely ill. Jesus' healing of the boy was John's second sign.

JOHN 4:46–54

46 Once more he visited Cana in Galilee, where he had turned the water into wine. And there was a certain royal official whose son lay sick at Capernaum. **47** When this man heard that Jesus had arrived in Galilee from Judea, he went to him and begged him to come and heal his son, who was close to death.

48 "Unless you people see miraculous signs and wonders," Jesus told him, "you will never believe."

49 The royal official said, "Sir, come down before my child dies."

50 Jesus replied, "You may go. Your son will live."

The man took Jesus at his word and departed. **51** While he was still on the way, his servants met him with the news that his boy was living. **52** When he inquired as to the time when his son got better, they said to him, "The fever left him yesterday at the seventh hour."

53 Then the father realized that this was the exact time at which Jesus had said to him, "Your son will live." So he and all his household believed.

54 This was the second miraculous sign that Jesus performed, having come from Judea to Galilee.

Jesus Returns to Cana in Galilee (4:43–47)

Galilee was home to Jesus and most of the twelve disciples. The Synoptic Gospels record many events in Galilee, but John chose not to duplicate their stories. Although most of John's focus was in Jerusalem and Judea, some record is given to Jesus' ministry in Galilee. Jesus' first miracle, called a sign, was performed in Cana of Galilee (2:1–11). John wrote after that event that Jesus "revealed his glory and his disciples put their faith in him" (2:11). Jesus visited Cana, about ten miles west of the Sea of Galilee and four miles north of Nazareth, after his visit with the Samaritan woman (4:1–42).

Jesus had experienced hostility in Galilee. When he spoke in the synagogue at Nazareth, he reminded the Jews that God had favor on people other than Jews (Luke 4:16–30). The worshipers at the synagogue wanted to kill him. John may have alluded to this event when he wrote: "Jesus himself had pointed out that a prophet has no honor in his own country" (John 4:44). However, Jesus' current trip in Galilee was going well. Jesus was welcome. People had been in Jerusalem for the Passover, and they remembered him well and warmly.

Jesus received an unnamed royal official while in Cana. The official, presumably in the court of King Herod, had heard of Jesus and made the long walk to Cana from Capernaum to ask Jesus to heal his son. The father did not believe the boy could live much longer. The father may have thought Jesus was his only hope. The man begged Jesus to come to Capernaum to heal his boy.

Most of us have known people who *get religion* during a crisis. In my experience, most of these have turned out to be empty promises. When the situation was reversed, they went back to living just as they did before—without any apparent commitment to God or to the church. The royal official was different.

Jesus Heals a Royal Official's Son (4:48–50)

The people of Galilee were probably similar to those in Jerusalem in that many of them came to him just because of his miracles. John noted that "Jesus would not entrust himself to them" (2:24). In Galilee, Jesus said, "Unless you people see miraculous signs and wonders, you will never believe" (4:48). "You" is plural, indicating that Jesus was talking not only to the man but to others who were nearby.

Jesus did not perform "signs and wonders" simply to attract attention. In the Old Testament, God acknowledged that to use more signs and wonders to try to persuade Pharaoh to let the children of Israel leave Egypt would not do any good (Exodus 7:3–4). Perhaps the Galileans were hoping for Jesus to heal someone or do some other miracle, but Jesus was not in the entertainment business.

Entertainment and recreation are important to us. Although such activities are not sinful in and of themselves, we live in a society that wants instant gratification, continuous pleasure, and little sacrifice. Worship never needs to be boring and tedious. Even so, like Jesus, the church is not in the entertainment business. People were attracted to Jesus, expecting a show, but Jesus distanced himself from that.

The royal official was not there to see "signs and wonders." He begged Jesus to see his son: "sir, come down before my child dies" (John 4:49). Consider the unusual nature of the scene. A man accustomed to all the trappings of the king's palace is pleading with a traveling rabbi from Nazareth to come and heal his son. Jesus had talked with one of the smartest men in the room in Jerusalem and a most unusual Samaritan woman in Capernaum. Now, a royal official stood before Jesus. Imagine what this series of events must have meant to the disciples as confirming signs of the identity of Jesus.

Jesus did not travel to Capernaum to heal the boy in response to the royal official's request. God does not always do things our way, although he will always act in our best interest. Jesus healed the boy from a distance. His word was simple, "You may go. You son will live" (4:50). John's use of details enhances his purpose in writing: "that you may believe that Jesus is the Christ" (20:30–31). I'm sure there was a lot of happiness in that moment, but all the royal official had to go on was the word of Jesus. The royal official thought that was enough.

The Meaning of the Sign (4:50–54)

The royal official believed. He asked for a miracle and he received it, although he did not know it until the next day. If that had happened to us, we would have made a cell phone call immediately. *How's my son?* I would have asked. But, that was not the world of the royal official. Even so, "the man took Jesus at his word and departed" (4:50).

Believing faith was to *take Jesus at his word.* The man had enough confidence and trust in Jesus that he did what Jesus said. Recall Jesus' first sign at Cana. The wedding party ran out of wine, and Mary, Jesus' mother, intervened. After she spoke with Jesus, she told those putting on the reception, "do whatever he tells you" (2:5), and they did. It is not enough to hear and know; genuine faith acts on what we have heard and known.

On the royal official's way home, he was met by some of his servants with good news: the boy was alive and improving. The man asked when it happened and then realized it was exactly the time that Jesus said "your son will live." At this point, it appears that the royal official explained what happened and when. As the servants heard the story, they must have been overwhelmed, for the Scripture says, "he and all his household believed" (4:53).

The royal official had his prayer answered, and his testimony of what happened changed the lives of those who lived and worked with him. It was truly a *faith-healing*, done without fanfare or the applause of the crowd. Jesus healed, not for entertainment purposes or to drum up financial support, but because he wanted to do so.

John commented that this was the second miraculous sign Jesus did in Cana. The sign was similar to the first; someone acted in faith on the word of Jesus. Good results happened at both signs. At the first sign, turning water into wine preserved the celebration at the wedding feast. On one level, this act reminds us that God came to make life better and more enjoyable. It further teaches that Jesus is the fulfillment of all God's previous revelation was meant to be. The second sign reminds us that God has power over sin, sickness, and death. Jesus had the power to heal and work a miracle even if he was many miles away from the boy. This sign would later encourage belief in Jesus' life, death, and resurrection, and in the transforming effect he can have in bringing life to all who believe.

Meaning for Today

Jesus knew miracles often attracted people for the wrong reasons, but God is not averse to miracles. The first great act of the Bible, creation, was a miracle. The life of Jesus was framed by miracle—his birth to Mary and his res-urrection from the grave. Since then, we have seen the miracles of new births and renewed relationships.

Today, we may pray for miracles, for healing and help. Sometimes we pray and do not get the answer we want, and then we overlook the many miracles we have already had. We may be like the royal official's son and the servants back home—we may have no idea that we have had experiences in which God is at work.

It is okay to ask for a miracle, and God always answers. God may say *yes, no, not yet,* or *be patient.* But, when God answers positively, it always is a miracle. It may be a direct miracle that changes your life. Most often, it is a miracle of grace, where God gives you the power to cope with life as it is, regardless of what happens. Either way, we can be sure God is acting in our best interest (Romans 8:28). Our role is to continue to live by faith. We take God at his word, and we trust him. We let God's grace spill over into our relationships to others, so that others will know that our faith is real and our God cares for us.

SIGNS AND FAITH

John's purpose was to tell the story of Jesus and his many "signs" in order that people might believe that Jesus is the Christ (John 20:30–31). Seven signs can be seen in the Gospel of John, but Jesus did many others. Signs reveal who Jesus is and what he was doing. The Savior of the world turned water into wine and healed a young boy.

These physical events became signs, for they revealed the life-changing and eternal consequences of faith in Jesus.

Jesus rejected a faith that was based only on signs and wonders (4:48). Real faith trusts in the word and person of Jesus and acts on it. Although the royal official's servants did not understand how the boy was healed, once they heard the testimony of the father, they too believed. The healing of the boy was the divine confirmation (a sign) of the royal official's faith. Belief does not mean we always get our way, but faith enables the understanding of what God is doing.

A Ministry of Healing and Praying

A royal official's faith led to the healing of his son; however, his journey of faith could not have happened unless someone cared for his son while he was seeking Jesus. Today, hospitals begun by religious institutions build on Jesus' ministry of healing. Pray for the caregivers, both within families and among those employed in these hospitals. Thank God for these healing institutions, but also consider how God can use you and your fellow class members to be an answer to prayer for sick people and their caregivers.

QUESTIONS

1. Have you had an experience that seemed to be a sign, pointing you to greater trust in Jesus Christ?

2. In what areas of life do you best *take Jesus at his word*?

3. In what areas of life have you ignored the need to *take Jesus at his word*?

4. Are you concerned enough about someone to
   continually seek Jesus for his or her welfare?

5. How can you do a more effective job in helping
   others deal with sickness and death?

—— U N I T T W O ——
Signs and Feasts
Showing Jesus' Identity

This unit is a study of John 5—12. It emphasizes especially Jesus' revelation of his identity through signs and the interpretation of those signs. At the same, it shows how Jesus revealed who he was in actions and teachings in the context of four festivals of the Jews. These festivals include the weekly Sabbath in John 5; and the annual festivals of Passover in John 6, Booths (also called Tabernacles) in John 7—8, and Dedication (Hanukkah) in John 10:22–39.[1]

Lesson 10	Seeing and Believing	John 9:1–41
Lesson 11	Decision Time	John 10:22–42
Lesson 12	The Resurrection and the Life	John 11:14–53
Lesson 13	The Climactic Moment	John 11:55–57; 12:20–37, 44–50

NOTES

1. Unless otherwise indicated, all Scripture quotations in unit 2, lessons 7–8 and 12–13, are from the New International Version; and all Scripture quotations in unit 2, lessons 9–11, are from the New American Standard Bible (1995 edition).

LESSON SEVEN

Who's in Charge Here?

MAIN IDEA

Jesus' healing the man on the Sabbath showed his authority based on his unique relationship with the Father as God's Son.

QUESTION TO EXPLORE

In what ways do you acknowledge Jesus' authority in your life?

STUDY AIM

To explain the controversy over Jesus' healing on the Sabbath and to acknowledge Jesus' full authority in my life today

QUICK READ

Jesus healed the lame man on the Sabbath and defended himself against attacks made by religious leaders, saying that he had been sent by God.

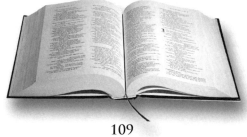

In many cases, having a set of rules is a good thing. Without specific guidelines, everything from our legal system to a leisurely game of baseball on a Saturday afternoon would be dramatically affected.

Sometimes, though, rules get in the way more than they help. For example, sometimes rules may be made arbitrarily. Likewise, sometimes people press rules to illogical and unintended limits. When this happens it is called *legalism*.

This very thing—legalism—was happening in Jesus' day. During his ministry Jesus challenged some of the popular notions of what it meant to be religious. Moreover, he maintained that he had the authority to make these challenges because of his unique relationship to God.

JOHN 5:1–24, 31–40

1 Some time later, Jesus went up to Jerusalem for a feast of the Jews. **2** Now there is in Jerusalem near the Sheep Gate a pool, which in Aramaic is called Bethesda and which is surrounded by five covered colonnades. **3** Here a great number of disabled people used to lie—the blind, the lame, the paralyzed. **5** One who was there had been an invalid for thirty-eight years. **6** When Jesus saw him lying there and learned that he had been in this condition for a long time, he asked him, "Do you want to get well?"

7 "Sir," the invalid replied, "I have no one to help me into the pool when the water is stirred. While I am trying to get in, someone else goes down ahead of me."

8 Then Jesus said to him, "Get up! Pick up your mat and walk." **9** At once the man was cured; he picked up his mat and walked.

The day on which this took place was a Sabbath, **10** and so the Jews said to the man who had been healed, "It is the Sabbath; the law forbids you to carry your mat."

11 But he replied, "The man who made me well said to me, 'Pick up your mat and walk.' "

12 So they asked him, "Who is this fellow who told you to pick it up and walk?"

13 The man who was healed had no idea who it was, for Jesus had slipped away into the crowd that was there.

14 Later Jesus found him at the temple and said to him, "See, you are well again. Stop sinning or something worse may happen to you." **15** The man went away and told the Jews that it was Jesus who had made him well.

16 So, because Jesus was doing these things on the Sabbath, the Jews persecuted him. **17** Jesus said to them, "My Father is always at his work to this very day, and I, too, am working." **18** For this reason the Jews tried all the harder to kill him; not only was he breaking the Sabbath, but he was even calling God his own Father, making himself equal with God.

19 Jesus gave them this answer: "I tell you the truth, the Son can do nothing by himself; he can do only what he sees his Father doing, because whatever the Father does the Son also does. **20** For the Father loves the Son and shows him all he does. Yes, to your amazement he will show him even greater things than these. **21** For just as the Father raises the dead and gives them life, even so the Son gives life to whom he is pleased to give it. **22** Moreover, the Father judges no one, but has entrusted all judgment to the Son, **23** that all may honor the Son just as they honor the Father. He who does not honor the Son does not honor the Father, who sent him.

24 "I tell you the truth, whoever hears my word and believes him who sent me has eternal life and will not be condemned; he has crossed over from death to life.

•   •   •   •   •   •   •   •   •   •   •   •   •   •   •   •   •   •   •   •

31 "If I testify about myself, my testimony is not valid. **32** There is another who testifies in my favor, and I know that his testimony about me is valid.

33 "You have sent to John and he has testified to the truth. **34** Not that I accept human testimony; but I mention it that you may be saved. **35** John was a lamp that burned and gave light, and you chose for a time to enjoy his light.

36 "I have testimony weightier than that of John. For the very work that the Father has given me to finish, and which I am doing, testifies that the Father has sent me. **37** And the Father who sent me has himself testified concerning me. You have never heard his voice nor seen his form, **38** nor does his word dwell in you, for you do not believe the one he sent. **39** You diligently study the Scriptures because you think that by them you possess eternal life. These are the Scriptures that testify about me, **40** yet you refuse to come to me to have life.

Jesus at the Pool Called Bethesda (5:1–8)

Although we are not told which festival it was, verse 1 says that Jesus went up to Jerusalem "for a feast of the Jews." The Jewish people celebrated several religious festivals during the year. John 5—10 shows us Jesus' actions in the context of four of these festivals. The Gospel of John records the unknown festival here in John 5, the Feast of the Passover in John 6 (see 6:4), the Feast of Tabernacles (also called the Feast of Booths) in John 7—8 (see 7:2), and the celebration of Hanukkah in John 10 (see 10:22). A description of the first three festivals can be found in Leviticus 23.[1] Also, note that signs three through six are contained in John 5—10. The seventh sign in John's Gospel is found in John 11. Although the word "sign" is not used, the miracle found in this chapter is considered by many Bible students to be the third sign.

Verses 2–3 paint a picture for the reader. We are told about a pool called Bethesda near "the Sheep Gate." The pool was surrounded by five colonnades or porches. We are given another bit of information. This was an area in which the sick gathered day after day. It was a scene of grand beauty and architecture coupled with unimaginable suffering and hopelessness. Hopelessness would certainly characterize this man who had been lame for thirty-eight years. Some have noted that thirty-eight years was not much longer than the average life expectancy in the ancient world.[2]

It is interesting that Jesus would ask the paralyzed man the question in verse 6, "Do you want to get well?" In response to Jesus' question, the man gave the obvious explanation for why he had not been healed already. He had no one to assist him into the pool "when the water is stirred," and someone else entered in before him. Jesus did not respond directly to the man's explanation but instead ordered the man, "Get up! Pick up your mat and walk." The man's healing would not come through a splash in a pool, but rather through the word of the Son of God.

Controversy over the Healing (5:9–15)

The Gospel of John skillfully spins the story off in a new direction by telling us that these events occurred on a Sabbath day. At first the Jews were not upset because Jesus *healed* on the Sabbath. Rather, the Jews were upset with Jesus for instructing the healed man to carry his mat while he walked. The Jews pressed the commandment about the Sabbath to such unreasonable limits that they often missed the intended spirit of the law. Be aware that nowhere in the Old Testament does it say that it is illegal to carry one's mat on the Sabbath. This man broke Jewish tradition rather than the actual law of Moses.

While both Jesus and the man whom Jesus healed were Jewish, verses 10 and 15 describe Jesus' opponents as "the Jews." The word *Jew* or *Jews* in the New Testament often is used not merely to designate nationality but a particular religious perspective. That is, "the Jews" were those who strictly held to the old order of things. On the other hand, Jesus and his disciples, while being Jewish themselves, expressed a new religious identity. This new religious movement would eventually come to be known as Christianity.

Verse 14 tells of the second meeting of Jesus and the lame man. What Jesus said to him during this meeting comprises one of Jesus' most intriguing statements in all of the New Testament: "See, you are well again. Stop sinning or something worse may happen to you" (John 6:14). Some have interpreted this verse to mean that Jesus was drawing a direct link between sin and sickness. However, Jesus' words in John 9:3 and in Luke 13:2–5 seem to contradict this connection. Others have interpreted Jesus' words here as pointing beyond the physical into the eternal (see Mark 2:1–12). It should not escape us that healing was not the first thing Jesus mentioned in that story. Rather, Jesus said, "Son, your sins are forgiven" (Mark 2:5). Although the man in Mark 2 could not walk, he had a deeper, more profound problem. His sin separated him from God.

Moreover, in John 5:14 Jesus was not likely linking sinfulness with physical illness. On the contrary, he was likely linking sinfulness with an eternal, spiritual death.

The Jews Persecute Jesus (5:16–24)

After his second meeting with Jesus, the healed man was able to identify Jesus as the man who healed him. Verse 16 states that the Jews persecuted Jesus "because Jesus was doing these things on the Sabbath." If the Jews were upset with Jesus before, they became even more enraged because of the way in which Jesus countered their charge against him. In verse 17 Jesus made three claims: God is always at his work (implying that even God works on the Sabbath); the God of Abraham, Isaac, and Jacob is Jesus' Father; and because Jesus' Father was at work, Jesus must be at work also.

In verses 19–24 Jesus tried to correct any possible misunderstanding. Jesus was not trying to put himself over and above God. Instead, he emphasized his very dependence *on* God. For example, Jesus said that he could do nothing by himself (5:19), that his work was dependent on what the Father showed him must be done (5:19–20), and that the Father sent him into the world (5:23). Later on in verse 30 Jesus would state his dependence on the Father again: "By myself I can do nothing." Jesus was totally dependent on God. Nevertheless, Jesus the Son has the authority to do and say what he does (heal on the Sabbath, forgive people's sins, etc.) because of the special relationship he has to God the Father (see 1:1–14, 18).

Testimony Concerning Jesus (5:31–40)

Jesus, a human being, was teaching that he is the very Son of God. Jesus himself realized just how astonishing his claim is. This is why he told the Jews not to take his word for it, but to listen to those who testify in his favor. In John 5:31–40 Jesus listed four witnesses who gave testimony to his identity as the Son of God. These witnesses are John the Baptist (5:33–35); Jesus' works (5:36); God the Father (5:39); and the Scriptures (5:45).

John the Baptist's testimony about Jesus is recorded in John 1:19–34. John the Baptist told the priests, Levites, and Pharisees who came to question him that One would come after him. This One to come after was the "Lamb of God, who takes away the sin of the world!" (John 1:29). Although John the Baptist pointed to Jesus as the Messiah, the Jews rejected his testimony. John the Baptist was popular for a little while but was eventually beheaded.

On several occasions Jesus pointed to the miracles he performed as evidence he was the Son of God. The idea was that Jesus' signs were to help validate what he said. Jesus pointed to his miracles to validate his claims again later in the Gospel of John (10:25, 38; 14:11). We find this kind of witness given to another of God's messengers. Centuries earlier, when Moses had concerns about the Hebrews not believing what he said, God gave Moses three specific miracles to perform for the people so that they might believe (Exodus 4:1–9).

What did Jesus mean about the Father bearing witness to him (John 5:37)? Although the story is not recorded in John, some think Jesus might have been referring to God giving his blessing at Jesus' baptism (Mark 1:11). (God did this again during the transfiguration. See Matthew 17:1–8; Mark 9:2–8; Luke 9:28–36.) Others link the Father's testimony with that of the Scriptures, since they come from God.

The Jewish people took the study of Scripture very seriously. Many committed large portions of Scripture to memory, especially the first five books of the Old Testament. However, what so many of them failed to realize was that the words they cherished so much pointed forward to something much greater. It is astounding that a people who held the Scriptures in such high esteem failed to grasp their full meaning.

Implications and Actions

Isn't it hard to believe the Jewish religious leaders were so shortsighted? Even though so many things pointed to Jesus' authority, they refused to acknowledge Jesus' authority in their lives. And aren't there so many in the church today who still refuse to fully accept Jesus' authority in their lives, not to mention the rejection of Jesus that we find in the larger culture?

It can be quite easy to wag our fingers at those people in Scripture who got it all wrong. Perhaps it is satisfying to express a condescending *tisk, tisk* at our fellow Christians for failing to acknowledge Jesus' authority in their lives. However, as delightful as it may be to point out the shortcomings of others, God calls us to examine ourselves. If we are not attentive to our relationship with Christ, we may find ourselves rejecting him more frequently than we realize.

Christ calls us to accept him fully as Lord. We are called to accept his authority not only when it is convenient but also when it may go against everything we have ever known. It is in these latter instances that we must be sure that we are not rejecting him.

MISSING VERSES

Most Bible translations omit John 5:3b–4, perhaps putting them in a footnote, for they are not included in the earliest and best manuscripts of John's Gospel. These verses were probably added to later copies of John's Gospel to explain the legend of the pool near the sheep gate to future generations who didn't know about the legend.

APPLYING THIS LESSON TO YOUR DAILY WALK

- Try to identify some religious rules that you may tend to press over into legalism.

- Pray for God to reveal those areas in your life that you have not submitted to his authority.

- Reflect on those occasions where the authority of Christ was confirmed in your heart.

QUESTIONS

1. Legalism still exists in religion today. Why do you think people so often get bogged down by strict and often meaningless rules?

2. Out of all of the witnesses to the person of Jesus as God's Son, which do you think you would have found the most convincing (the testimony of John the Baptist; Jesus' miracles; God's testimony; the testimony of Scripture)? Why?

3. What is the area in your life that you find most difficult to give over to the authority of Jesus?

NOTES ───────────────────────────────────

1. The Feast of Hanukkah or Dedication was instituted during the time between the Testaments to commemorate the dedication of the temple after its defilement by Antiochus Epiphanes in the second century B.C. See lesson 11 on John 10:22–42.

2. See Lesley Adkins and Roy A. Adkins, *Handbook to Life in Ancient Rome* (New York: Oxford University Press, 1998), 341

LESSON EIGHT

Hungry for . . . ?

MAIN IDEA

Jesus' feeding of the 5,000 and his walking on water show he truly is the "living bread" who uniquely and supremely has the words of eternal life.

QUESTION TO EXPLORE

To whom besides Jesus can we go for eternal life?

STUDY AIM

To describe how Jesus' feeding the 5,000 and his walking on water relate to his identity as the bread of life and to commit myself fully to Jesus' lordship

QUICK READ

Jesus provided food for 5,000 people, walked on water, and taught the people that he is the bread from heaven who can give eternal life.

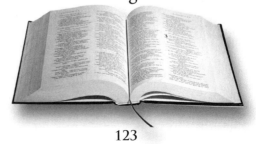

Nothing lasts forever. It doesn't take very long to find out just how true this saying is. That new bicycle we loved so much as a child may now be in someone's junk pile. Our clothes get stained, faded, or too small. A brand-new vehicle soon gets that first dreaded scratch and rolls over 100,000 miles before we know it. We learn it all too soon: *Nothing lasts forever.*

The same can be said about the spiritual life. We live in a world where people are searching for fulfillment. Too often people try to fill their lives with meaning only to find they're running on empty again. That with which they have tried to fill themselves has evaporated, and they soon find they are left longing to be filled again.

Jesus changes all of that. Jesus promises food that endures to eternal life.

JOHN 6:1–20, 25–35, 48–51, 66–69

1 Some time after this, Jesus crossed to the far shore of the Sea of Galilee (that is, the Sea of Tiberias), **2** and a great crowd of people followed him because they saw the miraculous signs he had performed on the sick. **3** Then Jesus went up on a mountainside and sat down with his disciples. **4** The Jewish Passover Feast was near.

5 When Jesus looked up and saw a great crowd coming toward him, he said to Philip, "Where shall we buy bread for these people to eat?" **6** He asked this only to test him, for he already had in mind what he was going to do.

7 Philip answered him, "Eight months' wages would not buy enough bread for each one to have a bite!"

8 Another of his disciples, Andrew, Simon Peter's brother, spoke up, **9** "Here is a boy with five small barley loaves and two small fish, but how far will they go among so many?"

10 Jesus said, "Have the people sit down." There was plenty of grass in that place, and the men sat down, about five thousand of them. **11** Jesus then took the loaves, gave thanks, and distributed to those who were seated as much as they wanted. He did the same with the fish.

12 When they had all had enough to eat, he said to his disciples, "Gather the pieces that are left over. Let nothing be wasted." **13** So they gathered them and filled twelve baskets with the pieces of the five barley loaves left over by those who had eaten.

14 After the people saw the miraculous sign that Jesus did, they began to say, "Surely this is the Prophet who is to come into the world." **15** Jesus, knowing that they intended to come and make him king by force, withdrew again to a mountain by himself.

16 When evening came, his disciples went down to the lake, **17** where they got into a boat and set off across the lake for Capernaum. By now it was dark, and Jesus had not yet joined them. **18** A strong wind was blowing and the waters grew rough. **19** When they had rowed three or three and a half miles, they saw Jesus approaching the boat, walking on the water; and they were terrified. **20** But he said to them, "It is I; don't be afraid."

• • • • • • • • • • • • • • • • • • • •

25 When they found him on the other side of the lake, they asked him, "Rabbi, when did you get here?"

26 Jesus answered, "I tell you the truth, you are looking for me, not because you saw miraculous signs but because you ate the loaves and had your fill. **27** Do not work for food that spoils, but for food that endures to eternal life, which the Son of Man will give you. On him God the Father has placed his seal of approval."

28 Then they asked him, "What must we do to do the works God requires?"

29 Jesus answered, "The work of God is this: to believe in the one he has sent."

30 So they asked him, "What miraculous sign then will you give that we may see it and believe you? What will you do? **31** Our forefathers ate the manna in the desert; as it is written: 'He gave them bread from heaven to eat.'"

32 Jesus said to them, "I tell you the truth, it is not Moses who has given you the bread from heaven, but it is my Father who gives you the true bread from heaven. **33** For the bread of God is he who comes down from heaven and gives life to the world."

34 "Sir," they said, "from now on give us this bread."

35 Then Jesus declared, "I am the bread of life. He who comes to me will never go hungry, and he who believes in me will never be thirsty.

•   •   •   •   •   •   •   •   •   •   •   •   •   •   •   •   •   •   •   •

48 I am the bread of life. **49** Your forefathers ate the manna in the desert, yet they died. **50** But here is the bread that comes down from heaven, which a man may eat and not die. **51** I am the living bread that came down from heaven. If anyone eats of this bread, he will live forever. This bread is my flesh, which I will give for the life of the world."

•   •   •   •   •   •   •   •   •   •   •   •   •   •   •   •   •   •   •   •

66 From this time many of his disciples turned back and no longer followed him.
67 "You do not want to leave too, do you?" Jesus asked the Twelve.
68 Simon Peter answered him, "Lord, to whom shall we go? You have the words of eternal life. **69** We believe and know that you are the Holy One of God."

Serving Up the Bread, Walking on the Water (6:1–20)

By this point in John's Gospel many people were following Jesus because of the signs he was performing among the people. The sign Jesus performed in John 6 is one of the miracles of Jesus that is recorded in all four Gospels. The sign is the feeding of the 5,000.

John 6:4 tells that the Festival of the Passover was near when this miracle took place. The Feast of the Passover was held by the Jews to commemorate God's powerful deliverance of the Israelites from the land of Egypt. An important part of the Passover celebration was that the Jews were supposed to eat unleavened bread for seven days. Thus, it is significant that after feeding the 5,000 with literal bread Jesus claimed to be the bread of life. Once again Jesus was teaching that he is above anything and everything found in Judaism. Jesus asserted in John 5 that he is more important than the Sabbath. In John 4, he showed that he is more important than holy places. In John 3, Jesus indicated that he was above the leading teacher, Nicodemus. In John 2 Jesus demonstrated that the purity he brought went beyond the old purification rituals found in Judaism.

After witnessing the miraculous sign of Jesus multiplying the bread and the fish, the crowd began discussing Jesus' identity. They stated, "Surely this is the Prophet who is to come into the world" (John 6:14). This saying is a reference to Deuteronomy 18:15–18. For some time the common belief among the Jews was that God would one day raise up a prophet like Moses. Indeed, in John 1:17–18 we are told that Jesus is greater than Moses. This prophet to come would serve as a king to the people of Israel and deliver them from their surrounding political enemies. This was precisely why Jesus withdrew to a mountain at the height of the crowd's excitement. They wanted a king to forever provide them with literal bread and literal protection from their enemies. Jesus' intention, however, was to point beyond the physical needs of the people. He is the answer, not merely to their physical need, but to their spiritual need.

If the disciples had any doubt about who Jesus was, their misunderstanding would be corrected again when Jesus performed what many consider to be the fifth sign recorded in John's Gospel. As the disciples rowed hard against the choppy sea, they suddenly noticed Jesus walking *on* the sea!

Jesus then identified himself to the frightened group of disciples. The way Jesus identified himself is significant. In Greek, "It is I" literally means *I am.* "I AM" is how God had referred to himself in Exodus 3:13–14. Therefore, while on one level Jesus was simply identifying himself to his disciples, on another level Jesus was identifying himself as the person who is one with God the Father.

Jesus Is the Bread of Life (6:25–35, 48–51)

Although Jesus and his disciples had "set off across the lake for Capernaum" (John 6:16), it did not take the crowd long to find them again (6:25). Jesus immediately pointed out the crowd's real motive for searching for him. The crowd was still thinking only of the physical. They had come to Jesus because they wanted their bellies filled again and had failed to grasp the significance of the miracle that was performed in their midst.

At this point in the narrative Jesus began to point to himself as the bread of life. In verse 27 Jesus told the crowd not to "work for food that spoils, but for food that endures to eternal life, which the Son of Man will give you." Jesus went on to tell the crowd that the work God requires is to believe in the one God has sent (John 6:29). Thus, Jesus pointed to himself as the food that endures to eternal life. Yet again Jesus was teaching that the crowds should believe in him because he had been sent by God.

The crowd's response to Jesus is nothing less than remarkable. After Jesus told them they should believe in him, they asked him to perform a miracle to back up the claim that God had sent him. This was the same crowd for whom Jesus miraculously provided food the day before. On the other hand, the crowd may have been asking for a miracle or sign that was more specific. Scholars tell us that the Jews believed that the messiah would be able to provide manna from heaven just as Moses had done. This is probably the intent behind verse 31. However, Jesus was quick to correct the crowd's interpretation of the manna provided to the Hebrews in the wilderness. Jesus reminded them that it was not Moses who provided them with bread, but God. Just as God provided literal bread then, so it was the Father who gave them "the true bread from heaven" now (6:32). This bread gives life to the world. Just like the woman at the well in John 4:15, the crowd was still focused on the physical. They imagined literal bread.

"I am the bread of life," Jesus told the crowd, trying to clue them in to the metaphor (6:35). Again, Jesus pointed to God the Father. Jesus had not come to express his own agenda, but to do the work God sent him to do. God's will is that the world believe in the Son and receive eternal life.

As usual "the Jews" were not impressed by what Jesus said (6:41). They did not view Jesus as the Son of God but merely as the son of Joseph. In their view, this poor young man grew up to be a lunatic, or worse—a blasphemer. After all, he was claiming to be "the bread from heaven." Jesus warned them to stop their grumbling and persisted in making his radical claim (6:43): Those who are truly of God will come to Jesus and accept him.

Finally, Jesus told the crowd plainly who he is and called attention to the inferiority of the bread that came to the Hebrews in Moses' day, thereby placing himself above Judaism. In the days of Moses the Hebrews were filled with bread but became hungry again. To the contrary, those who partake of Jesus, the bread of life, will never hunger again. They will live forever. This eternal life will come at great cost, however. Eternal life would become available to the world through Jesus' sacrifice of his own flesh on the cross.

To Whom Shall We Go? (6:66–69)

Just as the crowd kept giving Jesus' words about bread from heaven a literal interpretation, so the Jews were confounded by Jesus saying that the bread from heaven is his flesh. Jesus did not try to correct their misunderstanding. He simply continued with the metaphor. Those who eat his flesh and drink his blood will gain eternal life, since these are real food and drink (John 6:55). Once again Jesus stated his dependence on the "living Father" and pointed out the supremacy of the new, living bread opposed to the old manna that left people wanting more (6:57).

Verse 60 tells us that at this point even some of Jesus' disciples became troubled by Jesus' words. A hard teaching though it may be, Jesus said that the words he had spoken are Spirit and life. Human hearts and minds are dull. Even when the message of the gospel is spoken plainly, we are in need of God's illuminating presence to guide us into all truth.

In verse 66 we are told that many of Jesus' disciples turned back and no longer followed him. Jesus had gone too far. What he said was too hard.

Our churches often communicate the ease of the Christian life. To be sure, a relationship with Jesus does mean that we can cast all our cares upon him. Indeed, Jesus' yoke is easy and his burden is light (Matthew 11:30). John 6:66, however, reminds us of the radical call Jesus has placed on our lives. We are called to a fulltime commitment of trust and obedience.

We must not deceive ourselves. There are some hard things in the Christian faith: hard teachings, difficult expectations, vexing struggles. At times some of us may find the question in verse 67 humming on the edge of our minds, "You do not want to leave too, do you?" This hum of uncertainty must be drowned out by the same roaring response Peter first gave (6:68): "Lord, to whom shall we go?"

Although the road of discipleship may become difficult, we must be ever mindful that this Savior we follow has the words of eternal life. He is "the Holy One of God" (6:69), or, to go back to something John has already told us in John 1, Jesus is "God the One and only," who makes the Father known (1:18). This is our Jesus. This is our confession.

Implications and Actions

It can be easy to be distracted, even tempted, by the voices that clamor for our attention in today's world. Many of these voices claim to have the answers to life's most difficult mysteries or the secret to a life of fulfillment.

In the midst of this storm of voices we must look up to see Jesus walking over and above them all. It is Jesus who uniquely and supremely has the words of eternal life.

When we begin to feel the deep hunger pangs of a restless soul, that deep spiritual thirst that the world's goods cannot quench, let us bring our attention back to the true bread from heaven—Jesus, the bread of life.

PASSOVER

On the tenth day of the first month each man was to take a year-old male lamb without defect. On the fourteenth day of the same month these lambs were to be slaughtered at twilight, but none of the animal's bones were to be broken.

During the first Passover the blood of the lamb was smeared on the top and sides of the doorframes of the homes of the Hebrews. A later development was that the blood of the lamb was sprinkled on the altar in the temple (see 2 Chronicles 35:1–19). Each family was to eat the meat of their lamb after it had been roasted over a fire. The meat was not to be boiled or eaten raw, and none of it was to be left over until morning. The meat was eaten with unleavened bread and bitter herbs. For seven days the Hebrews were to eat unleavened bread "because it was on this very day that I brought your divisions out of Egypt" (Exodus 12:17). The Israelites were supposed to celebrate the Passover every year.

CASE STUDY

A friend says, *I think Jesus said a lot of good things, but I don't really believe you have to believe in Jesus to know God. I think you can be on good terms with God without Jesus.* With John 6 in mind, how would you respond to this person?

QUESTIONS

1. "What must we do to do the works God requires" (John 6:28)?

2. How would you explain to someone Jesus' words in verse 35 about never going hungry and never being thirsty?

3. Why do you think Jesus didn't try to give further explanation to the Jews about what he really meant when he talked about people eating his flesh and drinking his blood?

4. Jesus said that his words are "spirit" and "life" (6:63). What are some of your favorite words of Jesus? Why?

LESSON NINE

Conflict over Jesus

MAIN IDEA

Jesus' encounters at the Feast of
Booths show that his claim to be
from God forces a decision as to
whether people will accept him
and his offer of genuine life.

QUESTION TO EXPLORE

What have you decided about
who Jesus is and whether
he is worth your life?

STUDY AIM

To summarize Jesus' encounters at
the Feast of Booths and to affirm my
commitment to who Jesus truly is

QUICK READ

During Jesus' dramatic appearance
and public teaching at the Feast of
Booths, different groups struggled
with Jesus' identity as the Messiah.

Our reaction to Jesus is in a different category from the ordinary decisions of our lives. Some decisions have minor effects that are soon forgotten, but our decision about Jesus affects every aspect of our lives and for all eternity. In John 7, paragraph after paragraph finds people struggling to decide about Jesus.[1]

JOHN 7:1–31, 37–43

[1] After these things Jesus was walking in Galilee, for He was unwilling to walk in Judea because the Jews were seeking to kill Him. [2] Now the feast of the Jews, the Feast of Booths, was near. [3] Therefore His brothers said to Him, "Leave here and go into Judea, so that Your disciples also may see Your works which You are doing. [4] "For no one does anything in secret when he himself seeks to be known publicly. If You do these things, show Yourself to the world." [5] For not even His brothers were believing in Him. [6] So Jesus said to them, "My time is not yet here, but your time is always opportune. [7] "The world cannot hate you, but it hates Me because I testify of it, that its deeds are evil. [8] "Go up to the feast yourselves; I do not go up to this feast because My time has not yet fully come." [9] Having said these things to them, He stayed in Galilee.

[10] But when His brothers had gone up to the feast, then He Himself also went up, not publicly, but as if, in secret. [11]

So the Jews were seeking Him at the feast and were saying, "Where is He?" **12** There was much grumbling among the crowds concerning Him; some were saying, "He is a good man"; others were saying, "No, on the contrary, He leads the people astray." **13** Yet no one was speaking openly of Him for fear of the Jews.

14 But when it was now the midst of the feast Jesus went up into the temple, and began to teach. **15** The Jews then were astonished, saying, "How has this man become learned, having never been educated?"

16 So Jesus answered them and said, "My teaching is not Mine, but His who sent Me. **17** "If anyone is willing to do His will, he will know of the teaching, whether it is of God or whether I speak from Myself. **18** "He who speaks from himself seeks his own glory; but He who is seeking the glory of the One who sent Him, He is true, and there is no unrighteousness in Him. **19** "Did not Moses give you the Law, and yet none of you carries out the Law? Why do you seek to kill Me?" **20** The crowd answered, "You have a demon! Who seeks to kill You?" **21** Jesus answered them, "I did one deed, and you all marvel. **22** "For this reason Moses has given you circumcision (not because it is from Moses, but from the fathers), and on the Sabbath you circumcise a man. **23** "If a man receives circumcision on the Sabbath so that the Law of Moses will not be broken, are you angry with Me because I made an entire man well on the Sabbath? **24** "Do not judge according to appearance, but judge with righteous judgment."

25 So some of the people of Jerusalem were saying, "Is this not the man whom they are seeking to kill? **26** "Look, He is speaking publicly, and they are saying nothing to Him. The rulers do not really know that this is the Christ, do they? **27** "However, we know where this man is from; but whenever the Christ may come, no one knows where He is from." **28** Then Jesus cried out in the temple, teaching and saying, "You both know Me and know where I am from; and I have not come of Myself, but He who sent Me is true, whom you do not know. **29** "I know Him, because I am from Him, and He sent Me." **30** So they were seeking to seize Him; and no man laid his hand on Him, because His hour had not yet come. **31** But many of the crowd believed in Him; and they were saying, "When the Christ comes, He will not perform more signs than those which this man has, will He?"

• •

37 Now on the last day, the great day of the feast, Jesus stood and cried out, saying, "If anyone is thirsty, let him come to Me and drink. **38** "He who believes in Me, as the Scripture said, 'From his innermost being will flow rivers of living water.' " **39** But this He spoke of the Spirit, whom those who believed in Him were to receive; for the Spirit was not yet given, because Jesus was not yet glorified. **40** Some of the people therefore, when they heard these words, were saying, "This certainly is the Prophet." **41** Others were saying, "This is the Christ." Still others were saying,

"Surely the Christ is not going to come from Galilee, is He? **42** "Has not the Scripture said that the Christ comes from the descendants of David, and from Bethlehem, the village where David was?" **43** So a division occurred in the crowd because of Him.

Brotherly Advice (7:1–10)

The verses leading up to John 7 mark a significant shift in the arc of Jesus' popularity. To this point in John's Gospel, Jesus' acclaim had grown with the crowds, reaching a fever pitch following the feeding of the 5,000 (John 6:15). Some difficult and challenging teaching ensued. In John 6:66, we learn that Jesus' band of followers began to diminish.

John 7 opens approximately six months later with the approach of the Feast of Booths or Tabernacles. This week-long celebration commemorated the Exodus from Egypt. To reenact the wilderness wanderings of Exodus, pilgrims at the feast would stay in huts. It was the largest feast in first-century Jewish life and was sometimes simply referred to as *the feast*. This celebration coincided with the harvest and was a time of great rejoicing (see Leviticus 23:33–44).

Jesus' brothers encouraged him to return from Galilee to Judea to perform his works before the massive crowds that would have gathered for the feast. We learn in verse 5 that they did not believe in him, and so these words may reflect a certain sarcasm or cynicism. They may have been implying, *If you want to be a great leader, you'd better get to Jerusalem and replace the followers who've abandoned you.* Their disbelief at this point seems remarkable. Surely they had seen at least some of his miracles and heard the stories surrounding his birth. Even those who had known Jesus the longest were having doubts and rejecting his identity.

Jesus' response clearly contrasted their commitments with his. His words in verse 6, "My time is not yet here," echoed his words to his mother at the wedding feast in Cana, "My hour has not yet come" (John 2:4). Jesus' brothers did not understand divine timing because they were not committed to who Jesus was and what he was doing. The world could not hate them because, at that point, they had decided to align themselves with the world.

In a confusing turn of events, Jesus told them to go to Jerusalem while he remained in Galilee (7:8). Jesus said, "I do not go up to this feast" (7:8). Jesus then proceeded to go to Jerusalem in verse 10. This was not a case of Jesus being untruthful about his intentions. His brothers were urging him to go as a pilgrim to *keep*, or *celebrate*, the feast. Jesus entered Jerusalem mid-week (7:14), not to partake in the feast but to take the opportunity for teaching. His initial absence was noticed, however, with the pilgrims, the residents of Jerusalem, and the Jewish leadership debating his identity.

Grumbling and Opposition (7:11–31)

This section begins with the crowd grumbling and the Jews seeking Jesus during his absence. Jesus had been away from Jerusalem for some time, and these pilgrims were eager to see him first-hand. The opinion polls were split between the views that he was a force for good and that he was a false leader. The Jews, John's term for the religious leaders, had made up their mind to get rid of Jesus (5:16, 18), and they were plotting their strategies for their next encounter.

In this context, Jerusalem was packed with pilgrims, charged with emotions, and moving to the rhythms and worship of the ancient festival rites. Jesus stepped into this mix—commanding the religiously charged stage at the temple—and he began to teach. This was Jesus' first public teaching in Jerusalem recorded in John, and the religious leaders' plans of opposition were shattered in their stunned response to the quality of his teaching (7:15).

The Gospel of John does not record the content of Jesus' teaching here, but it gives us Jesus' reaction to their reaction. His teaching was from God. As a result, it was not the case that his competence as a teacher was to be debated or evaluated. Rather, their competence as hearers or listeners was at stake (7:17). His teaching forced a life decision—not an opinion or passing evaluation of his ability as a teacher.

In verse 19, Jesus abruptly addressed the plots against him, taking the crowd by surprise. They were unaware of the religious leaders' plans. The words about Moses, the Sabbath, and circumcision (7:21–24) point back to Jesus' Sabbath healing of the man at the pool of Bethesda (John 5). This event had sparked the resolve of the Jews to kill him (5:18). Jesus highlighted their inconsistency in criticizing that healing. They were willing to allow one law, regarding circumcision, to supersede their Sabbath laws. In healing the lame man, Jesus exercised a great act of mercy, making the man whole and relieving his suffering. He was not tearing down the Sabbath regulations but was rather fulfilling the point of the Sabbath.

In verses 25–31, the debates raged on. It almost appears that they were making a two-column balance sheet of pros and cons about Jesus as the Messiah. The residents of Jerusalem, who evidently knew about the plot against him, tried to reconcile his bold public teaching with the inaction of their leaders to stop it. Jesus' origin was more fodder for their discussions. While Herod's chief priests and scribes had been able to point to Bethlehem as the birthplace of the Messiah (Matthew 2), others in the first century expected the Messiah to appear full-grown, in a supernatural way.[2] These residents of Jerusalem evidently held some view along those lines. Jesus responded emphatically, shouting that his origin reached beyond any city of birth to the One who sent him. Again, Jesus threw the responsibility on his hearers. If they truly knew God, they would recognize God's servant.

Some in the crowd asked a very perceptive question. *What more could the Messiah do than what Jesus had done?* (7:31). So often in the Gospels, miracles and signs led to demands for more! Like our bottomless appetite for more possessions, more power, or more acclaim, we find a bottomless demand on the part of many for yet more *proof.* The decision about Jesus, however, must be an act of faith.

Decision Time (7:37–43)

Water was a key element in the celebration of the Feast of Booths. Each day, a priest would draw water from the pool of Siloam, and a special procession would march to the temple where it was poured around the altar. This reflected the miraculous provision of water from the rock in Exodus 17, the gratitude of the people for rain leading to the harvest, and prayer for rain for the coming year. One rabbi even taught that those who failed to celebrate the Feast of Tabernacles would have no rain in the next season![3]

At the height of the feast (perhaps at the time of the water procession), Jesus again demanded the attention of the massive crowds. While the typical posture for teaching was sitting down (see Matthew 5:1), Jesus stood and cried out. The water of life is not to be found at any pool, in any well (John 4:13–14), or at any feast. Jesus is the living water. He is the fulfillment of all that lies behind the great Feast of Booths. Note the shift in Jesus' words. He *is* the water for the thirsty, but he creates streams of water *in his believers.* Believing in him changes us. It creates an uncontainable overflow that does not stagnate or end in us but reaches out to others. John explained in 7:39 that this living water comes not from us but from the Holy Spirit in us.

Verses 40–43 capture the mystery of unbelief. The incarnate Word was among them. He had performed miracles, taught, and clearly pointed to his relationship with God. Some were willing to take the half-step of recognizing him as a prophet. Others were convinced, "This is the Christ" (7:41). Again, the issues of origin were raised, and some in the crowd were able to identify Bethlehem as the expected birthplace. Verse 43 summarizes not just the situation on the final day of the Feast of Booths, but the overall situation at that time, "So a division occurred in the crowd because of Him."

In the course of this chapter, various groups acted as if Jesus were on trial with themselves as the jury, debating the merits of his messianic case. In his responses however, Jesus turned the tables. As one commentator observed, "His trial becomes their trial."[4]

This Lesson and Life

Like the people in Jerusalem at the Feast of Booths, Jesus forces a decision on us. Will we accept that this man is the Son of God? C.S. Lewis famously crystallized the choices available to us when it comes to Christ. While many want to categorize Jesus as a great moral teacher (who might be studied and ignored), passages like this one remove that option. Lewis wrote,

A man who was merely a man and said the sort of things Jesus said would not be a great moral teacher. He would either be a lunatic—on a level with the man who says he is a poached egg—or else he would be the Devil of Hell. You must make your choice. Either this man was, and is, the Son of God: or else a madman or something worse. You can shut Him up for a fool, you can spit at Him and kill Him as a demon; or you can fall at His feet and call Him Lord and God. But let us not come with any patronising nonsense about his being a great human teacher. He has not left that open to us. He did not intend to.[5]

WATER AND THE FEAST OF TABERNACLES

The daily water ceremony at the Feast of Tabernacles had a controversial background. Leviticus 23:39–44 contains the original instructions for the feast, and it makes no mention of water. The use of water was added at a later date. The Sadducees and Pharisees came to disagree about where and how the water should be poured. While the former believed it should be poured on the ground around the altar, the latter claimed it should be poured on the altar and allowed to run down.

About 90 years before Jesus was born, the high priest, Alexander Jannaeus, followed the Sadducees' method. The pilgrims at the feast became enraged and threw citrons at him. (Citrons were also a traditional part of the feast.) Jannaeus ordered his soldiers to attack the crowd, and 6,000 Jews were killed.[6]

Jesus used the emotionally-charged ceremony of water, which in that case had led to death, and offered something much greater—living water. Throughout John's Gospel we find Jesus taking the great traditions, expectations, and symbols of Judaism and showing how God was fulfilling them or completing them in his life, death, and resurrection.

CASE STUDY

Once we have decided to accept Jesus as Lord, we are charged to tell others about his truth. Imagine a conversation with a skeptical co-worker or friend. The person responds to your testimony that while Jesus was a great teacher on par with other great religious leaders, he certainly was not divine. How would you respond from the events and teachings in John 7?

QUESTIONS

1. Given all that Jesus' brothers knew about Jesus, why would they *not* believe?

2. What are some objections people raise today about Jesus being the Christ?

3. What evidence would you use in telling others about Jesus as the Christ?

4. How do we tend to "judge according to appearances" (John 7:24)?

N O T E S

1. Unless otherwise indicated, all Scripture quotations in unit 2, lessons 9–11, are from the New American Standard Bible (1995 edition).

2. Leon Morris, *The Gospel According to John*, rev. ed. (Grand Rapids, Michigan: William B. Eerdmans, 1995), 365.

3. Morris, *John*, 372.

4. George R. Beasley-Murray, *John*, Word Biblical Commentary, vol. 36, 2nd ed. (Nashville: Thomas Nelson Publishers, 1999), 122.

5. C.S. Lewis, *Mere Christianity* (New York: Simon and Schuster, 1943), 56.

6. M.O. Wise, "Feasts," *Dictionary of Jesus and the Gospels*, ed. Joel B. Green, Scot McKnight, I. Howard Marshall (Downers Grove, Illinois: InterVarsity Press, 1992), 239.

FOCAL TEXT
John 9:1–41

BACKGROUND
John 8:12—9:41

LESSON TEN
Seeing and Believing

MAIN IDEA

Jesus' healing of the blind man shows that Jesus provides abundant life to all who will let him open their eyes.

QUESTION TO EXPLORE

How well do you see?

STUDY AIM

To trace the meaning of the conversation and the actions in Jesus' healing the blind man and to believe in Jesus as he did

QUICK READ

Jesus' healing of the blind man caused division among others. When it came to the truth about Jesus, the blind man gained true sight, while others chose blindness.

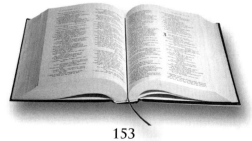

When you are trying to work, do you want or need light? It depends on your work. For the doctor, the photographer, the plumber, or the accountant, light is essential. It illuminates and reveals. It guides and it opens possibilities. For thieves or drug dealers, light exposes. It repels. It makes their work difficult or impossible.

In John 8:12, Jesus said, "I am the Light of the world." In chapter 9 we see reactions to the light. For some it illuminated. For others it blinded.

JOHN 9:1–41

1 As He passed by, He saw a man blind from birth. **2** And His disciples asked Him, "Rabbi, who sinned, this man or his parents, that he would be born blind?" **3** Jesus answered, "It was neither that this man sinned, nor his parents; but it was so that the works of God might be displayed in him. **4** "We must work the works of Him who sent Me as long as it is day; night is coming when no one can work. **5** "While I am in the world, I am the Light of the world." **6** When He had said this, He spat on the ground, and made clay of the spittle, and applied the clay to his eyes, **7** and said to him, "Go, wash in the pool of Siloam" (which is translated, Sent). So he went away and washed, and came back seeing. **8** Therefore the neighbors, and those who previously saw him as a beggar, were saying, "Is not this the one who used to sit and beg?" **9** Others were saying, "This is he," still others were saying, "No, but he is like him." He kept saying, "I am the one." **10** So they were saying to him, "How then were your eyes opened?" **11** He answered, "The man who is called Jesus made clay, and anointed my eyes, and said to me, 'Go to Siloam and wash'; so I went away and washed, and I received sight." **12** They said to him, "Where is He?" He said, "I do not know."

13 They brought to the Pharisees the man who was formerly blind. **14** Now it was a Sabbath on the day when Jesus made the clay and opened his eyes. **15** Then the Pharisees also were asking him again how he received his sight. And he said to them, "He applied clay to my eyes, and I washed, and I see."

16 Therefore some of the Pharisees were saying, "This man is not from God, because He does not keep the Sabbath." But others were saying, "How can a man who is a sinner perform such signs?" And there was a division among them. **17** So they said to the blind man again, "What do you say about Him, since He opened your eyes?" And he said, "He is a prophet." **18** The Jews then did not believe it of him, that he had been blind and had received sight, until they called the parents of the very one who had received his sight, **19** and questioned them, saying, "Is this your son, who you say was born blind? Then how does he now see?" **20** His parents answered them and said, "We know that this is our son, and that he was born blind; **21** but how he now sees, we do not know; or who opened his eyes, we do not know. Ask him; he is of age, he will speak for himself." **22** His parents said this because they were afraid of the Jews; for the Jews had already agreed that if anyone confessed Him to be Christ, he was to be put out of the synagogue. **23** For this reason his parents said, "He is of age; ask him."

24 So a second time they called the man who had been blind, and said to him, "Give glory to God; we know that this man is a sinner." **25** He then answered, "Whether He is a sinner, I do not know; one thing I do know, that though I was blind, now I see." **26** So they said to him, "What did He do to you? How did He open your eyes?" **27** He answered them, "I told you already and you did not listen; why do you want to hear it again? You do not want to become His disciples too, do you?" **28** They reviled him and said, "You are His disciple, but we are disciples of Moses. **29** "We know that God has spoken to Moses, but as for this man, we do not know where He is from." **30** The man answered and said to them, "Well, here is an amazing thing, that you do not know where He is from, and yet He opened my eyes. **31** "We know that God does not hear sinners; but if anyone is God-fearing and does His will, He hears him. **32** "Since the beginning of time it has never been heard that anyone opened the eyes of a person born blind. **33** "If this man were not from God, He could do nothing." **34** They answered him, "You were born entirely in sins, and are you teaching us?" So they put him out. **35** Jesus heard that they had put him out, and finding him, He said, "Do you believe in the Son of Man?" **36** He answered, "Who is He, Lord, that I may believe in Him?" **37** Jesus said to him, "You have

both seen Him, and He is the one who is talking with you."
38 And he said, "Lord, I believe." And he worshiped Him.
39 And Jesus said, "For judgment I came into this world,
so that those who do not see may see, and that those who
see may become blind." **40** Those of the Pharisees who
were with Him heard these things and said to Him, "We are
not blind too, are we?" **41** Jesus said to them, "If you were
blind, you would have no sin; but since you say, 'We see,'
your sin remains.

The Power of the Light (9:1–7)

John 9 opens without any markers of a significant change
in setting from John 7—8. As a result, the general view is
that these events likely took place in Jerusalem either on
the last day of the Feast of Booths (John 7:2–39) or in the
days immediately afterward.

In John 9:1, Jesus noticed a blind man, who almost
certainly would have been a beggar in their culture. The
disciples, somewhat rudely (he could hear, after all), made
a theological assumption about the source of his suffering.
Their question took for granted that some terrible sin was
in his past. This belief tapped a strain of Old Testament
theology (see Deuteronomy 11:13–17; Proverbs 3:33; 11:21).
Some exaggerated this line of thinking and reached the
over-simple conclusion, *You get what you deserve.* A man
blind from birth presented a special challenge to this

theology. It seemed severe to so punish a man for the sins of his parents. Some rabbis tried to evade this problem by suggesting that such a man committed sin in the womb![1] Jesus rejected the disciples' simplistic (and ultimately cruel) assumption about the source of his suffering and pointed instead to the man's need and to Jesus' opportunity to do God's work.

In John 9:5, Jesus repeated the great statement from the previous chapter, "I am the Light of the world" (John 8:12). Jesus' words about light, spoken at the end of the feast, carried special weight. He uttered the proclamation in the temple court. There huge lamps, visible across Jerusalem, had been lit each night of the feast. Those lamps had been extinguished, making Jesus' "I am the Light" statement all the more striking. He is the true light! The healing of the blind man is an elaboration of that great statement and an illustration of that power.

In the Gospels, Jesus healed many blind people.[2] Jesus chose to perform these miracles in various ways. In this case, he used spittle and mud to anoint the man's eyes. Jesus then sent him to wash in the pool of Siloam. To this point, we know almost nothing about the man. He had been a passive listener. Did he initially take offense at being the subject of a theological debate? Was he taken by surprise when the moist substance touched his eyes? Without elaboration, John reports that he obeyed and experienced sight—for the first time in his life. The subsequent passage takes a surprising turn as Jesus disappears from the scene for twenty-eight verses. This man takes center stage, and his character is remarkable.

Reactions to the Light (9:8–12)

Giving sight to the blind, although common with Jesus, is not so in the rest of Scripture. The only incident that comes close is Saul's recovery of sight in Acts 9. Several passages in the Old Testament refer to the giving of sight as a sign of the Messiah and as a divine activity (Exodus 4:11; Isaiah 29:18; 35:5; 42:7).

While we might expect such an unheard-of miracle to solidify public opinion regarding Jesus' identity, instead, we find continued division (John 7:43). The "Light of the world" illuminates and exposes. Some see, while others choose blindness. The man's neighbors and others in the community debated this miracle, with some convinced that this was not the same man. While Christians are at times chided for an irrational belief in miracles, we find in Scripture and in some skeptics today an irrational disbelief in miracles. Their prior assumption that the blind do not see caused many who saw the man to shut their eyes to the reality standing before them.

When asked what happened, the man testified in the simplest of terms. He narrated his change in life with one sentence, pointing to Jesus (whom he had not yet seen). Faced with this act of power beyond their comprehension, the neighbors took the man to the experts on things religious—the Pharisees (9:13).

Law and Order (9:13–34)

Jesus' already rocky relationship with the Pharisees had deteriorated significantly in chapters 7 and 8 (8:59). As a result, the Pharisees, blinded by their opposition, only heard in the report of this amazing miracle that a Sabbath violation had occurred. According to their interpretations, Jesus had committed several offenses. Making mud was classified as a form of kneading and mixing. Placing it on the eyes breached the prohibition of *anointing*. Healing of any form on the Sabbath was prohibited unless the person's life was in danger.[3] The division Jesus caused reached even the Pharisees, with some able to look beyond the supposed Sabbath breach to the unprecedented nature of what had happened. This minority opinion is silent for the rest of the chapter. However, as the opposition continued, the Pharisees launched an investigation and interrogation worthy of a modern crime drama.

The Pharisees started with the man who had been healed from his blindness. He again gave a straightforward, one-sentence summary of the miracle. We can detect their perplexity in their request for the man's opinion of Jesus (9:17). As the experts, the Pharisees were more accustomed to settling such matters themselves without the input of the uneducated. The man's identification of Jesus as a prophet was a bold testimony, placing Jesus in the highest religious position he knew. His eyes were opening wider!

The Pharisees' irrational disbelief led them to the same conclusion as some of the man's neighbors. Their line of thinking went something like this: (1) Since someone who violated their Sabbath interpretations could not be from God, and (2) since only someone from God could restore sight, then (3) surely the man had not been blind.

To check out his story they visited his parents (9:18–23). The parents appear significantly more cowed under questioning by the officials than did their son. Perhaps a lifetime of whispers about some sin on their part having caused the blindness had led them to distance themselves from their son. They conveyed the absolute minimum amount of information to the Pharisees, confirming his identity and his blindness but professing to know nothing more. Afraid of excommunication from the synagogue, they emphatically pointed the Pharisees back to their son. Notice that in the second part of the Pharisees' question, the Pharisees finally conceded the miracle, "How does he now see?" (9:19).

Undaunted in their zeal to discredit Jesus, the Pharisees returned to the man (9:24–34). Perhaps they were hoping to find inconsistencies in his testimony that would discredit him. They started with the command, "Give glory to God" (9:24). With their "we know," they were seeking to bully the man. They were saying something along the lines of, *We experts know that Jesus is a sinner. So you can tell the truth now.*

Ironically, the man did give glory to God in his simple testimony. He sliced though their circular arguments to express the heart of the matter and the facts of the case, "One thing I do know, that though I was blind, now I see" (9:25).

The Pharisees could say nothing new to such a profound statement. As a result, they simply asked the same questions again about how this came to be.

This man had summarized his story in so few words in the first place. He spoke plainly and clearly. He therefore assumed (perhaps ironically) that they wanted to follow Jesus. Notice the word "too" at the end of verse 27. His certainty about Jesus had grown to the point that the man, too, considered himself a disciple.

Appalled at the suggestion of following Jesus, the Pharisees testified that they followed Moses. They knew God worked through Moses, but they again raised the issue of Jesus' origin (7:27, 41–42). In response, this man of few words, who had spent his life as a beggar, spun together an argument that devastated the Pharisees' position. They were starting with their preconceived notions and working to explain away the events. He started with his first-hand experience and drew the obvious conclusion that this was a work of God. Unable to cope with his testimony, the Pharisees put him out of the synagogue (9:34).

Eyes Wide Open, Eyes Clamped Shut (9:35–41)

We do not know the setting or the context of Jesus' meeting with the man. Verse 35 simply says that Jesus heard of his punishment (and steadfastness) and sought him out. Jesus asked a simple question, "Do you believe in the Son of Man?" (9:35). This title is the favorite self-description of Jesus in the Gospels. The title stems from Daniel 7:13 and carries associations of divinity, the work of God, the people of Israel, and the Messiah. Not surprisingly, the man asked for clarification (John 9:36). Jesus poignantly referred to the man's new sight: "You have . . . seen Him" (9:37). In response, the man's eyes opened wider, and he is described as *worshipping* Jesus (9:38). He saw more clearly than anyone!

Jesus' teaching about having come for judgment (9:39) seems to contradict his words to Nicodemus in John 3:17. While salvation and bringing light are Jesus' purpose and mission, the reaction of others to the light brings judgment. In willful blindness they judge themselves. When Pharisees overhearing this statement asked about it, Jesus responded that their arrogance as teachers and as so-called experts removed any excuse. If they had the humility to accept their need for the light, then their eyes would be open. Claiming to see perfectly without need for Jesus, they revealed their blindness. Light illuminates. It also exposes.

This Lesson and Life

The formerly blind man repeated several times in this passage his story of meeting Jesus. He communicated it clearly and simply, whether he was talking to friends or foes. After we have experienced the "Light of the world," we need to be able to communicate that experience clearly. This communication does not need to be a theological treatise. The man in chapter 9 had not yet seen Jesus and knew very little about him. He could say without question, however, "This one thing I know" (9:25). We should be prepared to complete that sentence for friends, neighbors, coworkers, or skeptics. Our sentence might not be as dramatic as, "Though I was blind, now I see" (9:25), but the important thing is that it is *our* experience of hope, salvation, and peace that comes from meeting the "Light of the world."

DO WE GET WHAT WE DESERVE?

The strongest proponents in Scripture of a theology that chains together suffering with sin were Job's friends. Faced with Job's tremendous suffering, they espoused again and again the idea that Job must have done something truly wicked, and they urged him to repent. For example, Eliphaz claimed, "Who ever perished being innocent, or where were the upright destroyed? According to what I have seen, those who plow iniquity and those who sow trouble harvest it" (Job 4:7–8).

We know from Job 1, however, that other factors were at work. Likewise, Jesus saw something else at work in the man born blind. Whatever the cause, the man's blindness provided the opportunity for compassion and bringing glory to God.

Today we still hear echoes of *you get what you deserve* theology. Some still connect suffering with a lack of faith. Others tend to speculate following disasters about the sins of the affected nation or victims. Rather than piling condemnation on suffering, Jesus showed compassion and healing. God can turn suffering to glory!

CASE STUDY

It appears in John 9 that the man's parents had no interest in even exploring how their son's life had changed. Many believers today find it easier to talk about Jesus with friends or strangers than with family. How could you take steps to tell a non-believing family member about Jesus?

QUESTIONS ───────────────────────────────

1. How do you react to the suffering of others?

2. When have you experienced Jesus bringing division?

3. What kind of opposition do we face for our testimony?

4. In your life, how would you complete the man's sentence about experiencing Jesus: I once was _____, but now I _____?

NOTES

1. George R. Beasley-Murray, *John*, Word Biblical Commentary, vol. 36, 2nd ed. (Nashville: Thomas Nelson Publishers, 1999), 155.

2. Matthew 9:27–31; 12:22–23; 15:30–31; 21:14; Mark 8:22–26; 10:46–52; and Luke 7:21–22.

3. Leon Morris, *The Gospel According to John*, rev. ed. (Grand Rapids, Michigan: William B. Eerdmans, 1995), 427. To see how Jesus responded to such critiques, see John 5:15–21; Luke 6:5, 9; or Luke 13:15–16.

FOCAL TEXT

John 10:22–42

BACKGROUND

John 10:1–42

LESSON ELEVEN

Decision Time

MAIN IDEA

Jesus' insistence on his identity as God's Son challenges people to decide to believe in and follow him as sheep follow their shepherd.

QUESTION TO EXPLORE

What is it about Jesus that persuades you to believe in and follow him?

STUDY AIM

To trace the flow of thought in this passage of Scripture and to identify reasons for believing in and following Jesus

QUICK READ

In Jesus' encounter in the temple with the Jews at the Feast of Dedication, Jesus responded to their hostility with a clear statement of his relationship with the Father and with an invitation to believe.

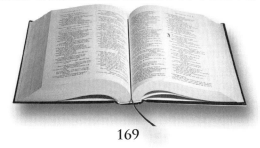

If you had lived in first-century Jerusalem, what would it have taken for you to believe in Jesus? Would a spectacular miracle have done it? Would teaching with knowledge and authority have done it? Would you have connected the prophecies and expectations from Scripture with Jesus, or would you have been too invested in the status quo to take an honest look? The discussion in the last half of John 10 climaxes with an invitation to believe.

JOHN 10:22–42

22 At that time the Feast of the Dedication took place at Jerusalem; **23** it was winter, and Jesus was walking in the temple in the portico of Solomon. **24** The Jews then gathered around Him, and were saying to Him, "How long will You keep us in suspense? If You are the Christ, tell us plainly." **25** Jesus answered them, "I told you, and you do not believe; the works that I do in My Father's name, these testify of Me. **26** "But you do not believe because you are not of My sheep. **27** "My sheep hear My voice, and I know them, and they follow Me; **28** and I give eternal life to them, and they will never perish; and no one will snatch them out of My hand. **29** "My Father, who has given them to Me, is greater than all; and no one is able to snatch them out of the Father's hand. **30** "I and the Father are one."

31 The Jews picked up stones again to stone Him. **32** Jesus answered them, "I showed you many good works from the

Father; for which of them are you stoning Me?" **33** The Jews answered Him, "For a good work we do not stone You, but for blasphemy; and because You, being a man, make Yourself out to be God." **34** Jesus answered them, "Has it not been written in your Law, 'I said, you are gods'? **35** "If he called them gods, to whom the word of God came (and the Scripture cannot be broken), **36** do you say of Him, whom the Father sanctified and sent into the world, 'You are blaspheming,' because I said, 'I am the Son of God'? **37** "If I do not do the works of My Father, do not believe Me; **38** but if I do them, though you do not believe Me, believe the works, so that you may know and understand that the Father is in Me, and I in the Father." **39** Therefore they were seeking again to seize Him, and He eluded their grasp.

40 And He went away again beyond the Jordan to the place where John was first baptizing, and He was staying there. **41** Many came to Him and were saying, "While John performed no sign, yet everything John said about this man was true." **42** Many believed in Him there.

A Celebration of Consecration (10:22)

The Gospel of John takes us forward by a couple of months to the celebration of the Feast of the Dedication. This is better known today as *Hanukkah.* Just as Jesus appropriated the imagery of the Feast of Tabernacles in the previous passage (John 9:1—10:21), he drew on the rich associations and history embodied in the Feast of the Dedication in this passage. Like Tabernacles, the Feast of the Dedication was an eight-day feast celebrated with much rejoicing. Unlike Tabernacles, the faithful could enjoy this feast outside of Jerusalem, but the pomp of the temple and the city proved a popular draw.

The Feast of the Dedication celebrated a most unlikely victory. The year 167 B.C. marked a low point for Israel. The Greek ruler, Antiochus Theos Epiphanes (the self-bestowed, latter two parts of his name meant, *god manifest*), desecrated the temple. Antiochus had sought to eliminate worship of Yahweh and to draw Jewish culture into Greek norms (a process called *Hellenization*). The Jews had predictably resisted. To complete his vision, he tore down the altar in the temple, replaced it with a pagan altar, and sacrificed a pig on it to *Jupiter Olympius*. This sacrifice was to be repeated on the twenty-fifth day of each month.[1]

To understand the impact of this, try to imagine a different outcome of World War II. Imagine the anguish of watching Hitler's tanks destroy the Lincoln Memorial and of seeing Hitler wipe his muddy boots on the Declaration of Independence. That might begin to approach for an American the degree of devastation felt by the Jews.

In response, a Jewish rebellion, led by Judas Maccabaeus, won a most surprising victory over Antiochus. In 164 B.C., the temple was rededicated to God, and each year the Feast of the Dedication commemorated this most recent deliverance of God's people. It was celebrated with lights, food, and joy. In Jesus' day, those celebrating the feast would have done so with a longing for further deliverance from the oppression of Rome.

A Loaded Question, an Explosive Answer (10:23–30)

In verse 23, Jesus was walking in the temple grounds at the "portico of Solomon" (perhaps finding shelter from the winter wind), when the Jews gathered around him. The Gospel of John uses the term "the Jews" for the religious establishment opposed to Jesus. The other Gospels tend to use the more specific titles of Pharisees, scribes, or lawyers when talking about these opponents. In this case, they appear to have encircled Jesus, perhaps in a threatening way, with a couple of challenges (10:24). Their "how long will You keep us in suspense" could also be translated as, "How long will You keep annoying/plaguing/provoking us."[2] Their second question, "If you are the Christ, tell us plainly," reveals that they understood the implications of Jesus' actions and teaching (10:24). Jesus had not, however, publicly proclaimed his messiahship. They wanted his words *on the record*, for they were building their case to discredit him.

In his response, Jesus did not succumb to their demand. Instead of making the public declaration on their terms, Jesus pointed them to what he had already said and done.

The reason they did not believe was that they were not part of his flock.

This shepherd/sheep imagery reflects Jesus' teaching in the first half of chapter 10. Those verses came at the conclusion of the events surrounding the healing of the blind man (John 9).

While John's Gospel does not contain Jesus' parables, the extended imagery of 10:1–18 functions like a parable. Jesus used two aspects of this image. First, he said, "I am the door of the sheep" (10:7). This "I am" statement (there are seven in John[3]) captures Jesus' role in God's plan for salvation. The second "I am" in these verses provides the background for Jesus' response in verses 26–29. "I am the good shepherd; the good shepherd lays down His life for the sheep" (10:11).

The "shepherd" imagery reaches still further back in Scripture and would have caught the attention of those present. The Old Testament certainly describes some significant shepherds, including David and Moses. Psalm 23 famously declares, "The Lord is my shepherd" (Psalm 23:1). One well-known Old Testament association with the language of shepherds is a prophecy in Ezekiel 34. Verses 1–10 of that chapter level a devastating critique at Israel's leaders. It culminates, "Thus says the Lord God, 'Behold, I am against the shepherds, and I will demand My sheep from them and make them cease from feeding sheep. . . . I will deliver My flock from their mouth . . ." (Ezekiel 34:10). In drawing on this imagery, Jesus both described his care and protection for his people and rebuked the religious leaders as embodiments of Ezekiel 34. God had sent a new shepherd—a good shepherd—for his sheep.

In John 10:26, Jesus stated that the Jewish leaders' failure to believe stemmed from their not belonging to his flock. Some interpret this as a statement reflecting a strong view of election. Later in this encounter, however, Jesus invited a response of belief (John 10:37–38). Jesus continued to reach out to his opponents, even as their opposition and hostility increased.

The picture Jesus painted of his relationship with his sheep is one of compassion, knowledge, and security. In driving toward Meeker, Colorado, several years ago, we encountered some ranchers moving their sheep from a field on one side of the highway to the other. Three men on horseback were ostensibly in charge, but their border collies did all the work. With ruthless efficiency, they nipped, barked, and nudged the sheep in the right direction. In minutes, the whole flock was across the road.

Jesus drew on a very different kind of relationship between shepherd and sheep. Back in 10:3–5, Jesus described the sheep knowing the voice of the shepherd and the shepherd knowing them by name. In this relationship, the sheep follow the shepherd. The religious leaders had heard Jesus' words and wanted to kill him, while his flock heard his words and willingly followed.

For those in Jesus' flock, verses 28–29 provide some of the greatest words of assurance in all of Scripture. For those who follow Christ, his grip is firm, and their hope is secure. This is not a life of decay or decline, for it is "eternal." Jesus does not promise freedom from difficulties, for the verb "to snatch" (10:29) suggests a violent attempt to rip us away. He does, however, assure that we rest in the hands of the most powerful One of all.

While Jesus had not given the Jews the *yes* or *no* answer they desired (10:24), verse 30 reaches past what they had even imagined. The reason Jesus' flock is so secure lies in the essential unity of God and Jesus. As one scholar commented, "They had asked Jesus for a plain statement of his messiahship, and they got more than they had bargained for."[4] For the reader of the Gospel of John, this idea has been expressed from the opening verses of the Gospel, but for Jesus' opponents these words sparked a violent reaction.

Reasons to Believe (10:31–39)

In all likelihood, the Jews would have never before heard anything like verse 30. Jesus' statement so incensed them that they were ready to execute him on the spot. Most English translations imply that they "picked up" stones to kill him, but the verb typically means that they *bore* (or *carried*) stones (10:31). Some scholars have speculated that they brought their own stones to the encounter, since Solomon's portico probably did not have them lying around.

Jesus calmly faced his would-be executioners. He threw them off balance with his question about which of the Father's good works they found offensive. They did not want to talk about works, but they rather made the first official accusation of blasphemy. In their view, Jesus claimed too much. Their statement in verse 33 reveals much about their relationship with Jesus. It is not that they misunderstood him. They understood his implications fairly clearly. Their failure came in not pausing to consider whether his claims were *true*.

Jesus answered this accusation with Scripture. He quoted from Psalm 82:6, a well-known passage among Jewish scholars because of debates regarding its meaning. This passage was likely referring to Israel's leaders or judges who were exercising (and misusing) a god-like and God-given power. In explaining this passage, Jesus used a *how much more* argument. If the psalmist could refer to these earthly judges as "gods" and, as Psalm 82:6 continues, "sons of the Most High," then how much more can those words apply to Jesus? Jesus repeated the idea that he was sent from the Father. He added the word "sanctified" or *consecrated* (John 10:36). This word carried special weight at the temple during the Feast of Dedication. The feast celebrated the re-consecration of the temple by human beings. Jesus claimed a greater consecration by the Father.

Jesus clinched his argument in verses 37–38 with what would be his final appeal to the Jews in Jerusalem. They should look at his works. If his works failed to resonate with what they knew about God, then they should by all means reject him. If his works, however, reflected God, then they should believe no matter what he said. In verse 39, they made their choice. They could not "grasp" (10:39) Jesus because he rested in the power of the "Father's hand" (10:29).

Withdrawal to the Wilderness (10:40–42)

Jesus left Jerusalem for a remote location on the other side of the Jordan. In Jerusalem, Jesus had performed the miraculous and spoken the truth, and those who should have known better sought to stone him. In the wilderness, at the spot where John first bore witness to Jesus, we find people streaming to Jesus and "believing" (10:42).

This Lesson and Life

In this passage, Jesus emphasized the importance of his *works*. He implored the Jews to look at the miracles he had done and to judge him by those. Beyond his miracles, we can see in this passage the integrity connecting his teaching and actions. "Love your enemies and pray for those who persecute you," Jesus said (Matthew 5:44). In the face of enemies ready to kill him, Jesus continued to offer them the invitation to believe.

Occasionally I see the bumper sticker, *Don't look at me, look at Jesus.* That captures something true. Jesus is the "author and perfecter of faith" (Hebrews 12:2). At the same time, we need to show integrity between belief and actions in life. Our works need to point to Christ so that our friends, neighbors, family, and coworkers might believe in the power of Jesus.

SECURITY OF THE BELIEVER

Once saved, always saved remains a popular expression of an important belief for Baptists. This view is also called *perseverance of the saints* or *security of the believer.*

Some of the earliest Baptists in the 1600s debated the implications of this belief. Thomas Helwys was the primary author of one of the very first statements of Baptist belief, "A Declaration of Faith of English People, 1611." It emphasizes the warnings against drifting from the faith: "But let all men have assurance, that iff they continew vnto the end, they shalbee saved."[5] The "First London Confession, 1644" expressed a stronger view of this security: "Those that have this pretious faith wrought in them by the Spirit, can never finally nor totally fall away . . . but shall be kept by the power of God to salvation."[6]

The New Testament balances warnings and assurance for followers of Jesus. When you need assurance that God is able to keep you, this passage and Romans 8:31–39 state most clearly the confidence we can have that no person or thing can separate us from the love of Christ.

WHAT DOES IT MEAN THAT AS CHRISTIANS WE ARE PART OF JESUS' FLOCK?

- We can have confidence in Jesus' care for us.

- We have a relationship of trust and knowledge with Jesus.

- We can be assured of what Jesus gives to us: eternal life and protection.

- We can know that there is not a person, power, or force who can take us away from God.

QUESTIONS

1. What does the imagery of Jesus as shepherd and Christians as flock mean to you?

2. What factors led you to believe in Jesus?

3. When you are sharing your faith, what are the reasons you can give that others should believe?

4. What kept the Jews in the passage from believing?

N O T E S

1. B.K. Waltke, "Antiochus IV Epiphanes," *The International Standard Bible Encyclopedia*, vol. one, ed Geoffrey W. Bromiley (Grand Rapids, Michigan: William B. Eerdmans, 1979), 145.

2. George R. Beasley-Murray, *John*, Word Biblical Commentary, vol. 36, 2nd ed. (Nashville: Thomas Nelson Publishers, 1999), 173

3. "I am the bread of life" (John 6:35, 41, 48, 51); "I am the Light of the world" (8:12; see 9:5); "I am the door of the sheep" (10:7, 9); "I am the good shepherd" (10:11, 14); "I am the resurrection and the life" (11:25); "I am the way, and the truth, and the life" (14:6); "I am the true vine" (15:1, 5).

4. Leon Morris, *The Gospel According to John*, rev. ed. (Grand Rapids, Michigan: William B. Eerdmans, 1995), 465.

5. Thomas Helwys, "A Declaration of Faith of English People, 1611," in *A Sourcebook for Baptist Heritage*, ed. H. Leon McBeth (Nashville: Broadman Press, 1990), 40.

6. "The First London Confession, 1644," in *A Sourcebook for Baptist Heritage*, ed. H. Leon McBeth (Nashville: Broadman Press, 1990), 49.

LESSON TWELVE
*The Resurrection
and the Life*

MAIN IDEA

Jesus' making Lazarus live again challenges us to respond to Jesus as the One who offers and is the resurrection and the life.

QUESTION TO EXPLORE

Do you trust Jesus to be *your* resurrection and *your* life?

STUDY AIM

To respond to Jesus as the One who offers and is the resurrection and the life

QUICK READ

The raising of Lazarus brought glory to God by pointing to the fact that Jesus has power over death. Jesus demonstrated that his authority over death is not only a future hope but also a present reality.

I often have the privilege of telling people the good news of Jesus Christ. But I also am often called on to tell people bad news.

Not long ago, I was visiting a man in the hospital, and he died while I was there. His son was present in the room, but his wife was not. It fell to me to go across the street to the retirement home where his wife lived to give her the bad news. It was a painful moment when she heard the news and we sat and wept together before making our way to the hospital room where her husband lay. It is never pleasant to relay bad news like that, but the fact is that people die and someone has to break the news.

Later that week, however, we stood in the cemetery and, surrounded by the graves of hundreds, I turned to John 11 and read the good news, "I am the resurrection and the life. He who believes in me will live . . ." (11:25).[1] In the midst of bad news, Jesus provides good news of his authority over death.

JOHN 11:14–53

14 So then he told them plainly, "Lazarus is dead, **15** and for your sake I am glad I was not there, so that you may believe. But let us go to him."

16 Then Thomas (called Didymus) said to the rest of the disciples, "Let us also go, that we may die with him."

17 On his arrival, Jesus found that Lazarus had already been in the tomb for four days. **18** Bethany was less than two miles from Jerusalem, **19** and many Jews had come to Martha and Mary to comfort them in the loss of their brother. **20** When Martha heard that Jesus was coming, she went out to meet him, but Mary stayed at home.

21 "Lord," Martha said to Jesus, "if you had been here, my brother would not have died. **22** But I know that even now God will give you whatever you ask."

23 Jesus said to her, "Your brother will rise again."

24 Martha answered, "I know he will rise again in the resurrection at the last day."

25 Jesus said to her, "I am the resurrection and the life. He who believes in me will live, even though he dies; **26** and whoever lives and believes in me will never die. Do you believe this?"

27 "Yes, Lord," she told him, "I believe that you are the Christ, the Son of God, who was to come into the world."

28 And after she had said this, she went back and called her sister Mary aside. "The Teacher is here," she said, "and is asking for you." **29** When Mary heard this, she got up quickly and went to him. **30** Now Jesus had not yet entered the village, but was still at the place where Martha had met him. **31** When the Jews who had been with Mary in the house, comforting her, noticed how quickly she got up and went out, they followed her, supposing she was going to the tomb to mourn there.

32 When Mary reached the place where Jesus was and saw him, she fell at his feet and said, "Lord, if you had been here, my brother would not have died."

33 When Jesus saw her weeping, and the Jews who had come along with her also weeping, he was deeply moved in spirit and troubled. **34** "Where have you laid him?" he asked.

"Come and see, Lord," they replied.

35 Jesus wept.

36 Then the Jews said, "See how he loved him!"

37 But some of them said, "Could not he who opened the eyes of the blind man have kept this man from dying?"

38 Jesus, once more deeply moved, came to the tomb. It was a cave with a stone laid across the entrance. **39** "Take away the stone," he said.

"But, Lord," said Martha, the sister of the dead man, "by this time there is a bad odor, for he has been there four days."

40 Then Jesus said, "Did I not tell you that if you believed, you would see the glory of God?"

41 So they took away the stone. Then Jesus looked up and said, "Father, I thank you that you have heard me. **42** I knew that you always hear me, but I said this for the benefit of the people standing here, that they may believe that you sent me."

43 When he had said this, Jesus called in a loud voice, "Lazarus, come out!" **44** The dead man came out, his hands and feet wrapped with strips of linen, and a cloth around his face.

Jesus said to them, "Take off the grave clothes and let him go."

45 Therefore many of the Jews who had come to visit Mary, and had seen what Jesus did, put their faith in him. **46** But some of them went to the Pharisees and told them what Jesus had done. **47** Then the chief priests and the Pharisees called a meeting of the Sanhedrin.

"What are we accomplishing?" they asked. "Here is this man performing many miraculous signs. **48** If we let him go on like this, everyone will believe in him, and then the Romans will come and take away both our place and our nation."

49 Then one of them, named Caiaphas, who was high priest that year, spoke up, "You know nothing at all! **50** You do not realize that it is better for you that one man die for the people than that the whole nation perish."

51 He did not say this on his own, but as high priest that year he prophesied that Jesus would die for the Jewish nation, **52** and not only for that nation but also for the scattered children of God, to bring them together and make them one. **53** So from that day on they plotted to take his life.

Where Is Jesus When You Need Him? (11:1–16)

Jesus and his disciples were on the other side of the Jordan River when they heard the bad news. They had left

Jerusalem in order to escape persecution from the Jewish leaders who tried to stone him.

The bad news was that Lazarus was sick. Lazarus and his sisters, Mary and Martha, were dear friends of Jesus, and they likely assumed that if they could get word to Jesus about Lazarus's illness, Jesus would come immediately. However, Jesus had other ideas. Strangely, Jesus did not come immediately to his friends when he heard the bad news. Instead, he stayed where he was for two more days.

"This sickness will not end in death," Jesus told the disciples (John 11:4). That is not exactly the kind of sympathetic response we want or expect from Jesus when we call on him for help. We expect Jesus to jump to our requests. When we are sick or in need and we call on Jesus to heal us and help us, we don't expect Jesus to say, *It won't kill you!*

But Jesus had something else in mind. Jesus announced that Lazarus's sickness would result in "God's glory so that God's Son may be glorified through it" (11:4). Jesus saw a greater goal than the healing of a sick man. Jesus saw an opportunity for God to be glorified, and that goal would not be reached unless Jesus waited.

In the meantime, Lazarus did in fact die. Jesus abruptly announced that they were going back to Judea despite the objections of the disciples. He used the euphemism of falling asleep to explain that Lazarus was dead and that he was going back to Judea to wake him up. But the disciples took Jesus literally. They could not see the point of going back to the danger of Judea if Lazarus was merely asleep. If Lazarus was sleeping, he was getting better without the help of the Lord.

So Jesus told them straight up, "Lazarus is dead" (11:14). It was bad news. But Jesus knew that good news was coming. The disciple Thomas, whom we usually remember as a doubter, demonstrated great faith by encouraging the others to follow Jesus even if it meant their own deaths. Thomas trusted Jesus even when it seemed like Jesus' actions did not make sense.

Is It Too Late for Hope? (11:17–32)

Jesus showed up too late for the funeral of Lazarus. His inexplicable delay plus travel time from the other side of the Jordan River to Bethany made him four days late. There was a popular belief (although not a biblical idea) that the soul of a person would linger around the body for two or three days, but by the fourth day all hope was lost. The person was dead. Jesus did not appear until the fourth day, when decomposition had begun and there was no more hope.

Understandably, Martha and Mary were upset. You can almost hear the anger in Martha's voice when she scolded Jesus, "Lord, if you had been here my brother would not have died" (11:21). Later Mary used the same words of disappointment. "Lord, if you had been here, my brother would not have died" (11:32). But Jesus had not been there. Lazarus had died, and now it was too late.

Jesus did give Martha one ray of hope. He told her that Lazarus would be raised from the dead. She assured Jesus of her own hope that one of these days Lazarus would rise from the grave, but certainly not until the end of time. Doesn't that sound like standard funeral fare? Think of the nice things we say to one another at such a time to make us feel better. *Yes*, we say as we gather around the casket during visitation at the funeral home, *one of these days we will be together again, when the last trumpet sounds, in the sweet by and by.* That truth is supposed to make us stop our grieving. But for now, it is too late. At least, that is how Martha understood what Jesus said.

But Jesus was not talking about some nebulous time in the future. He said, "I am the resurrection and the life" (11:25). Note that Jesus used the present tense, not the future tense. Jesus borrowed hope from the future and inserted it into the present. It is as if the future was already happening! It is like tearing out the last page of a novel and inserting it into the middle of the story. We already know how the story is going to end because the future is now! Our hope is not some hazy wishful thinking for the future; it is a present reality because in Jesus the future has happened!

Martha probably did not understand all that Jesus was saying, but nevertheless she responded with faith. She declared her belief that Jesus was the Christ, the Son of God.

No one has full understanding of the implications of resurrection life in Christ. Since we do not, our response should be the same as Martha's. We trust that Jesus is the Christ, the Son of God, and we believe that faith in him leads to eternal life.

What Is All This Weeping About? (11:33–44)

Grief is a natural, God-given response to loss regardless of our faith. Despite Jesus' assurance to Martha and despite her confession of faith, grief was still a reality.

Friends had come to grieve with Mary and Martha. Jesus saw them weeping. Scripture says that when he saw them weeping, he became "deeply moved in spirit and troubled" (11: 33). When they arrived at the tomb, the weeping did not cease. Even "Jesus wept" (11:35).

I have often wondered why Jesus wept. Jesus knew about resurrection. Jesus even knew he was about to raise Lazarus from the dead. If Jesus knew that in a few minutes Lazarus would walk out of the tomb alive, why was he weeping?

Read the text again. It says, "When Jesus saw her weeping and the Jews who had come along with her also weeping, he was deeply moved in spirit and troubled" (11:33). Jesus did not weep because Lazarus was dead.

Jesus wept because the people he loved were weeping. It broke his heart that they were broken-hearted.

A few years ago my oldest son's school teacher died. My son admired him. Although this person's death was tragic, I did not know him and had no special emotional attachment to him. I went into my son's room that evening to break the bad news to him. My son began to weep. Even though I had no real attachment to the man who died, I found I could not help weeping with my son. Truthfully, I was not weeping for the man who died. I was weeping because someone I loved was weeping for the man who died. I was broken-hearted because my son was broken-hearted.

I think that is why Jesus wept. Jesus was not weeping for Lazarus. Jesus understood that the power of God was greater than the power of death. Jesus wept because those he loved were weeping. I think Jesus still weeps with us when we weep, even though from his point of view, resurrection is a reality.

When Jesus commanded the stone to be rolled away, Martha expressed her doubts. Jesus then revealed to her the point of this whole event. He revealed why he waited before coming to visit. He revealed why he did not come and heal Lazarus earlier. The point was that by trusting Jesus, the glory of God would be revealed to them. Seeing God's glory was more important than healing a sick man.

Jesus raised Lazarus from the dead. Technically, the raising of Lazarus was not a *resurrection*. It was a *resuscitation.* Lazarus died again later. Only Jesus has experienced a resurrection because he did not die again. But the Bible assures us that Jesus was the first fruit of those who will experience resurrection (1 Corinthians 15:20). Trusting Jesus assures us that we will experience true resurrection as well.

The raising of Lazarus was the seventh sign in the Book of John, and it pointed to the fact that Jesus was indeed the Christ, the Son of God. It also pointed forward to Jesus' own resurrection. The raising of Lazarus shows us that hope for resurrection and life comes only through Jesus.

Then Why Not Believe? (11:45–53)

One would think that such a miraculous sign would convince everyone to believe in Jesus. Some did believe, but others reported these events to the authorities. The authorities were worried that if they did not put a stop to Jesus, the people would turn away from them and follow Jesus, whom they saw as a heretic. In order to hold on to their own power, they had to kill him.

The chief priest, Caiaphas, pronounced an unwitting truth when he said, "You do not realize that it is better for you that one man die for the people than that the whole nation perish" (John 11:49). He did not understand the deeper truth he uttered, but we know now that because

Jesus died and rose again people can have true resurrection and life.

Implications and Actions

When Jesus announced to Martha that he was the resurrection and life, he told her, "Whoever lives and believes in me will never die." Then Jesus asked, "Do you believe this?" (11:25). He still asks us this question. In a world where death and disease are all around us, do you believe Jesus is your hope for resurrection and life?

Martha answered well. "Yes, Lord, I believe that you are the Christ, the Son of God, who has come into the world" (11:27). If we believe Jesus has power over death and we trust him with our lives, we will know true resurrection and life.

DEATH, RESUSCITATION, AND RESURRECTION

On several occasions in the Bible, a dead person came back to life. In 2 Kings 4, Elisha raised the Shunammite woman's son from the dead. In Mark 5, Jesus raised the daughter of Jairus. In Luke 7, Jesus raised the son of a widow from the town of Nain. And of course there is the raising of Lazarus. All of these stories are technically known as resuscitations. They are miracles of raising a dead person, but the person died again later.

There has been only one resurrection, the resurrection of Jesus. A resurrection is when a person is raised from the dead and the person does not die again. Although Jesus is the only resurrection in history, his resurrection gives us assurance that God has power over death and the power to give eternal life.

WHAT TO SAY?

You have been asked to say a few words at the funeral of someone in your church. You will want to say something about the person's life and what the person meant to you. But you also want to give the family and friends comfort and hope. In light of John 11, what are some things you could say?

QUESTIONS

1. When you pray, does it frustrate you that Jesus does not always answer as quickly as you wish? In light of Jesus' delaying his visit to Martha and Mary when they asked him to come, why do you think the answer to prayer is sometimes delayed?

2. What is the role of grief in the life of a Christian? Does grief betray a lack of faith?

3. Why did Jesus weep if he knew Lazarus was about to be raised? Do you think his weeping comforted or disturbed Mary and Martha? How do you relate to the thought that Jesus weeps with us when we weep?

4. What do you think Jesus meant when he said, "I am the resurrection and the life"? Do you think there is significance to the fact he used the present tense as opposed to the future tense?

5. Why do you think the religious authorities were concerned about what Jesus had done? How did this event lead to the decision to put Jesus to death?

NOTES ——————————————————————

1. Unless otherwise indicated, all Scripture quotations in unit 2, lessons 12–13, are from the New International Version.

FOCAL TEXT
John 11:55–57;
12:20–37, 44–50

BACKGROUND
John 11:54—12:50

LESSON THIRTEEN
The Climactic Moment

MAIN IDEA

Jesus' revelation of himself to the point of even giving his life so as to draw all people to himself calls us to recognize his sacrifice and respond in gratitude to him.

QUESTION TO EXPLORE

What does Jesus' offering himself centuries ago mean for you today?

STUDY AIM

To tell the significance for my life of Jesus' offering himself to draw all people to him

QUICK READ

As Jesus faced impending death, he predicted he would be lifted up and draw all people to himself. His prediction was about the method of death by which he would be killed, but it also spoke to his exaltation as he willingly carried out God's will.

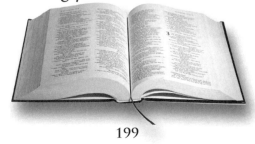

American culture celebrates success. Our history is filled with people who came to this land of opportunity with nothing and yet through hard work and true grit made a success of their lives. In fact, many people have become successful by writing books and leading seminars on *How to be Successful.*

Success is a religion for us. Indeed, even religion is celebrated when it is a success. In the business of religion, churches, preachers, and denominations are congratulated by their peers if baptisms are up, money is abundant, and attendance is growing. Religious leaders are deemed failures if their churches shrink or plateau.

The culture of success in the church seems a strange attitude for a religion that has a crucifixion as the climax of our faith. There is nothing successful about a crucifixion, at least not in this world. If anything, a cross was a symbol of shame and failure. In Jesus' case, the religious leaders were out to kill him, his followers were dropping off, and in the end, even his disciples abandoned him. But Jesus willfully and purposefully went toward the cross and claimed that when he was lifted up, it would draw all people to him.

JOHN 11:55–57

55 When it was almost time for the Jewish Passover, many went up from the country to Jerusalem for their ceremonial

cleansing before the Passover. **56** They kept looking for Jesus, and as they stood in the temple area they asked one another, "What do you think? Isn't he coming to the Feast at all?" **57** But the chief priests and Pharisees had given orders that if anyone found out where Jesus was, he should report it so that they might arrest him.

JOHN 12:20–37, 44–50

20 Now there were some Greeks among those who went up to worship at the Feast. **21** They came to Philip, who was from Bethsaida in Galilee, with a request. "Sir," they said, "we would like to see Jesus." **22** Philip went to tell Andrew; Andrew and Philip in turn told Jesus.

23 Jesus replied, "The hour has come for the Son of Man to be glorified. **24** I tell you the truth, unless a kernel of wheat falls to the ground and dies, it remains only a single seed. But if it dies, it produces many seeds. **25** The man who loves his life will lose it, while the man who hates his life in this world will keep it for eternal life. **26** Whoever serves me must follow me; and where I am, my servant also will be. My Father will honor the one who serves me.

27 "Now my heart is troubled, and what shall I say? 'Father, save me from this hour'? No, it was for this very reason I came to this hour. **28** Father, glorify your name!"

Then a voice came from heaven, "I have glorified it, and will glorify it again." **29** The crowd that was there and heard it said it had thundered; others said an angel had spoken to him.

30 Jesus said, "This voice was for your benefit, not mine. **31** Now is the time for judgment on this world; now the prince of this world will be driven out. **32** But I, when I am lifted up from the earth, will draw all men to myself." **33** He said this to show the kind of death he was going to die.

34 The crowd spoke up, "We have heard from the Law that the Christ will remain forever, so how can you say, 'The Son of Man must be lifted up'? Who is this 'Son of Man'?"

35 Then Jesus told them, "You are going to have the light just a little while longer. Walk while you have the light, before darkness overtakes you. The man who walks in the dark does not know where he is going. **36** Put your trust in the light while you have it, so that you may become sons of light." When he had finished speaking, Jesus left and hid himself from them.

37 Even after Jesus had done all these miraculous signs in their presence, they still would not believe in him.

• • • • • • • • • • • • • • • • • • • •

44 Then Jesus cried out, "When a man believes in me, he does not believe in me only, but in the one who sent me. **45** When he looks at me, he sees the one who sent me. **46** I have come into the world as a light, so that no one who believes in me should stay in darkness.

47 "As for the person who hears my words but does not keep them, I do not judge him. For I did not come to judge the world, but to save it. **48** There is a judge for the one who rejects me and does not accept my words; that very word which I spoke will condemn him at the last day. **49** For I did not speak of my own accord, but the Father who sent me commanded me what to say and how to say it. **50** I know that his command leads to eternal life. So whatever I say is just what the Father has told me to say."

The Plot of People (11:55–57)

Jesus was in trouble. He knew it, and everyone else knew it. After raising Lazarus from the dead, Jesus found it necessary to leave the area until the right time for him to completely reveal himself. Jesus' withdrawal was not a sign of cowardice. He knew that in the Father's plan, the hour for his death had not yet come.

Jesus returned to the danger zone when Passover time drew near. Passover was a sacred time when Jewish people came to Jerusalem from all over the world to celebrate and remember God's deliverance from slavery in Egypt. Evidently, Jesus normally came to Jerusalem for the Passover. But now Jesus was a wanted man; the religious leaders had already "plotted to take his life" (John 11:53). The rumors were flying. People wondered aloud whether Jesus would dare to show his face.

The chief priests and Pharisees had their spies out. The people were told that if anyone saw Jesus or knew where he was, they should report him so they could arrest him. Normally, such a situation is not a recipe for success. Normally, success requires staying out of jail and certainly out of the execution chamber. Normally, people will stay away from you if the authorities have their sights set on you. But in God's kingdom, things are seldom normal.

It is not that Jesus did not have any followers. Certainly there was Mary, Martha, and Lazarus, in whose house he stayed. Mary even gave Jesus a ridiculously expensive gift of perfume that she should have been saving for her dowry. Instead, she showed her devotion by pouring it all over Jesus' feet. Jesus said she was preparing him for burial.

The so-called triumphal entry into Jerusalem did bring out folks who celebrated Jesus' presence. Yet, Jesus came to town on a donkey instead of a steed. A donkey is hardly an appropriate animal for a successful and conquering king! Even in Jesus' parade of triumph, success seemed elusive.

The Plan of God (12:20–37)

Finally, the hour came when Jesus was ready to reveal himself to the world as the Messiah who would give his life as a sacrifice for others. Jesus' discussion of his impending death comes in the context of a request by "Greeks" to see Jesus (12:20).

The "Greeks" were not necessarily from Greece. This term was used for Gentiles who were steeped in the Greek culture of the day. Evidently these Gentiles were seekers, looking for life-meaning in the God of Israel. No doubt, they had studied and researched the other religions and philosophies of the day in their search for meaning. They had heard about Jesus and wanted to question him about his religious philosophy.

The Gospel of John uses this event to symbolize that the gospel is for the whole world, not just for Israel. John has already reminded us that God loved the world (3:16). Now Jesus was going to reveal God's plan for a crucified Christ not only to the Jews, but to the Gentiles as well.

If the Greeks were looking for Jesus to share his message with them, they were just in time. No sooner had they asked to see Jesus than Jesus said, "The hour has come for the Son of Man to be glorified" (12:23). Earlier in the Gospel of John, Jesus had stated that his "time" had not yet come.[1] But now the hour had come. Now it seemed as if Jesus was finally going to be successful.

But when Jesus said he was going to be "glorified," he meant he was going to be *crucified*. Jesus used an agricultural metaphor to describe his mission of death. As a seed cannot produce a fruit-bearing plant without separating itself from its source of life and being buried, so Jesus would be separated from life and be buried in order to bring life to others. His glory would come only by giving his life for the sake of the Father's will.

This truth goes beyond the voluntary death of Jesus. Jesus asserted that his followers must also give up their lives in service to Jesus if they want to experience true life in God's kingdom. Occasionally Jesus' followers must literally die for the sake of the kingdom. But most of the time it means followers must die to their own selfish desires for worldly success by serving others in Jesus' name. This may require giving our resources, abandoning our wishes, and sacrificing time and effort for the sake of others. Such a life may not make you successful by the cultural standards of this world, but it is the path to glory in God's kingdom.

This is difficult for most of us. It was even difficult for Jesus. Although he willingly gave his life for us, it did not prevent him from having a troubled heart. He knew the pain and sacrifice involved in following God's will. Yet Jesus was single-minded in his mission and did not allow the pain of personal sacrifice to override the will of the Father.

"A voice came from heaven," much like the voice that was heard at Jesus' baptism (John 12:28; see Mark 1:11). Some understood it to be the voice of an angel of God giving God's stamp of approval on what Jesus was about to endure. Others did not recognize the significance of the voice; they merely thought it thundered. There were, and always will be, those who understand God's work in Christ, and others who see nothing spectacular. Some understand why Jesus died for the sake of God's glory; others view the cross as nothing more than failure.

The crucifixion would be both painful humiliation and glorious exaltation. From the standpoint of the cultural norms of this world, the cross was humiliation and failure. But from God's standpoint, the cross was the completion of a mission of life and mercy that would result in eternal life and redemption for the whole world. Jesus asserted that when he was lifted up from the earth it would draw all people to him. There is double meaning here. He would be lifted up in humiliation and failure on a cross, but his sacrifice would be the ultimate gift of life for all people. He was successful only because he gave his life for us.

The Path for Success (12:44–50)

Jesus summarized his teachings by reminding his listeners that people need to come to a decision as to whether they are going to believe in him. They must decide whether looking at Jesus is the same as looking at the Father. They must decide whether they will keep the words of Jesus by humbling themselves through service rather than exalting themselves through worldly success.

Jesus came to save us, but people must decide whether to live in the darkness of the success models of this world or in the light of service for God's kingdom. By looking at the model Jesus gave, we can come to understand that it is only in following Jesus' example of sacrifice and service that we can find true life.

Implications and Actions

Do we need to take a new look at what it means to be a Christian? For most people, the purpose of religion is to find a faith that will provide some benefit for us in this world. We want a religion that will make us happy and successful, cure our diseases, and resolve our psychological foibles. We want Jesus to save marriages, fix finances, and help us live out the American dream.

But whenever religion gets easy or the gospel gets melted down to moral rules for better living, don't forget about the cross. While it is true that faith in Christ is the best way to live, the purpose of the gospel is not to make us more comfortable. The purpose of the gospel is to bring glory to God.

That is why Jesus willingly gave himself to be lifted up on a cross. There was nothing comfortable about it. The cross did not make him feel better. Jesus was concerned with one thing and one thing only: to bring glory to God by redeeming the world.

Followers of Jesus serve a similar purpose. It is not always easy. Often it requires great personal sacrifice. But when we follow the example of Jesus we will be successful in the kingdom of God. That is even better than achieving the American dream.

PASSOVER AND JESUS

The setting for this lesson is Passover. Passover was the holiday when the Jewish people celebrated and remembered their deliverance from slavery in Egypt during the time of Moses. On the day of Passover, the priest would sacrifice a lamb on the altar at the temple to symbolize the forgiveness of the sins of the people.

The Gospel of John goes to great lengths to connect the crucifixion of Christ with the slaughtering of the Passover lamb. In so doing, it declares Jesus as the Lamb of God who would take away the sins of the world (John 1:29). This important symbolism deepens our theological understanding of the sacrifice Jesus made. There is no longer a need for repeated animal sacrifices year after year. Jesus sacrificed himself for us once and for all (see Hebrews 9:26b).

HOW TO EXPLAIN?

Suppose you are talking to a young teenager about becoming a Christian. How would you explain how Jesus' sacrifice on the cross 2000 years ago affects the person's life now in the twenty-first century? What would you tell him or her about how following Jesus calls for sacrifice for the sake of God's kingdom?

QUESTIONS

1. How would you compare and contrast models of success in American culture with success in the kingdom of God?

2. What do you think the Greeks wanted to talk to Jesus about? If you had a chance to talk face to face with Jesus, what questions would you ask him about this incident?

3. How does it make you feel to read in John 12:27 that Jesus' heart was troubled? Have you ever pondered how Jesus felt when he was facing his death?

4. Why do you think people in the crowd reacted differently when they heard the voice from heaven? If they all heard the same thing, why did they have various interpretations of what it meant? What did Jesus mean when he said the voice was for their benefit, not his (12:30)?

5. Can you think of examples of a Christian sacrificing himself or herself for the sake of the kingdom?

N O T E S ——————————————————————————

1. See John 2:4; 7:6, 8, 30.

CHRISTMAS LESSON
Jesus, God with Us

MAIN IDEA

Jesus, who is God with us,
came to bring salvation.

QUESTION TO EXPLORE

What does Jesus' birth mean?

STUDY AIM

To explain the meaning of Jesus'
birth and to testify of how it
speaks to my life personally

QUICK READ

Jesus was born to be the Savior. As the
Savior, Jesus brings God's presence
into our lives and enables us to be
freed to serve him faithfully and freely.

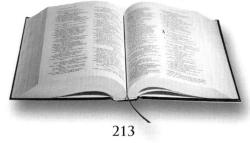

In these days, ordinary events tend to be given a lot of *hype* and shouted about to make them seem extraordinary. In contrast, the truly extraordinary birth of Jesus, "God with us," seems stated in a low-key manner, quite different from how a promoter would handle it today. "This is how the birth of Jesus Christ came about," the Gospel of Matthew states simply (Matthew 1:18).[1]

As you study the Scripture passage for this lesson, pay attention again to the simple story of "how the birth of Jesus Christ came about" and consider the extraordinary meaning it offers.

MATTHEW 1:18–25

18 This is how the birth of Jesus Christ came about: His mother Mary was pledged to be married to Joseph, but before they came together, she was found to be with child through the Holy Spirit. **19** Because Joseph her husband was a righteous man and did not want to expose her to public disgrace, he had in mind to divorce her quietly.

20 But after he had considered this, an angel of the Lord appeared to him in a dream and said, "Joseph son of David, do not be afraid to take Mary home as your wife, because what is conceived in her is from the Holy Spirit. **21** She will give birth to a son, and you are to give him the name Jesus, because he will save his people from their sins."

22 All this took place to fulfill what the Lord had said through the prophet: **23** "The virgin will be with child and will give birth to a son, and they will call him Immanuel"—which means, "God with us."

24 When Joseph woke up, he did what the angel of the Lord had commanded him and took Mary home as his wife. **25** But he had no union with her until she gave birth to a son. And he gave him the name Jesus.

Mary and Joseph—a Marriage Made in Heaven

Matthew 1 begins with the genealogy of Jesus, tracing his lineage from Abraham through David to a man named Joseph. Although we will see that Joseph was not the biological father of Jesus, Joseph was recognized as the legal father of Jesus. Even Jesus' critics recognized Joseph's status. Since Matthew was especially interested in affirming Jesus as the Messiah, this genealogical connection to Joseph was important.

Once Joseph is introduced, however, his bloodline takes second place to his character. He is called "a righteous man," meaning that he kept the law faithfully. Joseph and Mary had entered the traditional Jewish marriage arrangement. Their families had arranged for them to marry, thus beginning a period of engagement. Then Joseph and Mary had entered into betrothal, a formal time of a year or so in which they grew to know each other better but without sexual relationships. During the time of betrothal, two unusual experiences with angels shaped their lives.

Mary had a visit from an angel, telling her that she was pregnant (Luke 1:26–38). The encounter was unsettling, to say the least. She asked the angel how this could be, since she had no relations with a man. The angel said it was a work of God. God had started the birth process in her. Mary's response is classic. She was afraid and skeptical. The angel told her that nothing is impossible to God. Then Mary submitted herself to God's will and told the angel: "I am the Lord's servant. . . . May it be to me as you have said" (Luke 1:38).

At some point, Mary must have told Joseph that she was pregnant. We do not know how much Mary told him, but he must have thought in human terms, *She's pregnant. I didn't do it.* Mary's explanation to him was not enough. Joseph still cared for Mary, but he began to plan how to end their relationship without causing further hardship to her. But then one night, Joseph had a heavenly dream. An angel told him not to worry about taking her for his wife, for God had begun the birth process, not a man (Matt. 1:21–23). Joseph also found out who the baby really was. At some point, Joseph and Mary were married, the third step in traditional Jewish marriage rites.

The Gospel of Luke focuses on Mary's role in Jesus' birth, and the Gospel of Matthew focuses on Joseph's. Joseph had the option to deal tragically with Mary when he realized she was pregnant, but he did not. Even before the angel appeared to him, the righteous Joseph had already decided to deal with the situation quietly, not wanting to inflict any shame on Mary. But, when the angel appeared to him, Joseph had all the information he needed.

Through the angel, Joseph saw Mary as one who was honored by God. Mary may have told him that the Holy Spirit had begun the birth process, but now he really believed it. He heard that she would give birth to a son and that he would be named "Jesus." The angel even defined for Joseph what the name meant in regard to the purpose of his son's life, "he will save his people from their sins" (1:21). That information must have been staggering. But when the angelic dream was ended, Joseph "did what the angel of the Lord had commanded him and took Mary home as his wife" (1:24).

A common theme in the experience of both Mary and Joseph was that once they had heard the angel's information, they decided to believe and obey. They could have done otherwise, but they chose to follow God's will, honor each other, and become the human nurturing family in which Jesus grew to manhood.

Jesus, the Unique Son on Earth

Jesus is called three names in this lesson's Scripture: "Jesus," "Christ," and "Immanuel." The Gospel of Matthew begins with the words, "A record of the genealogy of Jesus Christ" (1:1), and then the birth story of Jesus begins with "This is how the birth of Jesus Christ came about" (1:18). Early in the church's history, the words "Jesus" and "Christ" were linked as one. "Christ" means *the anointed one.* "Christ" is the Greek equivalent to the Hebrew word *Messiah.* Matthew's Gospel emphasizes that making that Messianic connection is important, and it uses many Old Testament quotations to reinforce its importance to its Jewish-Christian readers.

"Immanuel" means "God with us" (1:23). The story of Jesus begins with the recognition that God is in our midst as "Immanuel." The Gospel of Matthew closes with the words that commission the church for its worldwide mission of making disciples (28:18–20). The empowering agent for that mission is the assurance from Jesus that he would also be with them. Indeed, Jesus said he would be with us "to the very end of the age" (28:20). God will be with us no matter where we go or how long we live.

"Jesus" is the Greek equivalent to the Hebrew word *Joshua,* which means *the Lord saves.* "Jesus" was a common name among Jewish children, but the firstborn son of Mary and Joseph gave it a unique quality that has transformed history. Jesus had a special purpose revealed in his name, "he will save his people from their sins" (1:21). From the Garden of Eden, God had been dealing with people who sinned. Sin was no surprise to God, for when he desired to create a people who would live in fellowship with him, he did not choose puppets on a string but free human beings who could walk *with* him or walk *away from* him. Even with sometimes rebellious people, God continued to work with them and ultimately provided a way through Jesus to deal with sin. The further unfolding of the Jesus story will tell how all of this happens, but for Christmas and Christians, the name "Jesus" teaches us that Jesus was born to save. Thanks be to God!

Jesus' birth has caused considerable interest for centuries. Some are fascinated by angelic visits, shepherds, wise men, and strange experiences with Elizabeth and Zechariah and the unusual birth of their son, John the Baptist. However, one theological issue that has elicited great response is the virgin birth. Mary first asked, "How can this be?" (Luke 1:34, NASB). Mary's question has been asked with differing meaning from scholars and lay people, skeptics and believers, *How can the virgin birth be?*

The angel quoted Isaiah 7:14 to Joseph, with emphasis on a virgin giving birth to a son and calling his name Immanuel. This statement must have comforted Joseph about Mary, but it also has become a focal point of much debate. Isaiah 7:14 foresees the birth of Ahaz's son, Hezekiah, eight centuries before Jesus. In the passing of time, the passage became a Messianic text that had meaning when it was said about Hezekiah but that finds ultimate fulfillment in Jesus. In Isaiah, the word in Hebrew for "virgin" can refer to a young woman who may

or may not be a virgin. The Hebrew word can be translated to a Greek word that means "virgin" and is so used in
the Greek Old Testament. Mary also referred to herself as
a "virgin" (Luke 1:34). The Gospel of Matthew obviously
follows the "virgin" translation, for it mentions in three
verses in this lesson's Scripture that Mary and Joseph had
no sexual relationships until after Jesus' birth. Jesus was
their firstborn, and then at least four more sons and two
daughters were born (Matt. 13:55).

Although word studies in Hebrew and Greek are helpful, these technical matters are less important to me than
some simpler impressions. For one thing, the virgin birth
is not a mirror of some crude impregnation of a helpless
young woman. No, the birth of Jesus is about the God
of this universe starting the birth process in a woman.
How can that be? Consider these points of background.
The first five words of the Bible are "In the beginning,
God created" (Genesis 1:1). Go to the life and ministry
of Jesus, and look at the astounding teaching and sometimes miraculous acts of Jesus. Consider Jesus' death on
the cross, burial in the grave, and resurrection. If I believe
these considerations, and I do, then why would I have any
problem believing God could start the birth process in
Mary? Is anything too difficult for God?

The Bible records other divine interventions in the birth
process, but they all had an earthly father and mother.
Jesus had no biological, earthly father, but he was born of
a woman. Theologically, the divine union of a heavenly

father and earthly mother provided Jesus with the unique *God-man* identity. The miraculous conception and virgin birth help us see the divine nature of Jesus, and the genealogy of Matthew emphasizes the human side. Jesus was fully God, fully human. The Gospel of John states, "The Word became flesh, and dwelt among us" (John 1:14, NASB).

Surely, this is still a great mystery, but have no fear of mystery. Mystery is not a problem to be solved but an awesomeness to be embraced. We were not created to know it all, but we know enough. God did not abandon the human race just because we sinned, but the fullness of God provided a way for us to experience his presence and deal with our sin. Through Jesus, we find our purpose in life and the enabling presence and power of God to fulfill it. Through Jesus, we have fellowship with God and one another.

For Life Today

Mary and Joseph were ordinary folks, largely unknown to the world. Yet, God used them and their faithfulness and obedience to change history. God still uses people like them today.

Let your knowledge of Jesus Christ and the enabling presence of Immanuel make a difference in the life of someone who does not have that knowledge or experience with Jesus Christ. Let your life be an extension of God to reach and minister to others who may have forgotten or do not know that the gospel is "good news of great joy that will be for all the people" (Luke 2:10).

JOHN'S CHRISTMAS STORY (JOHN 1:1–18)

The Gospel of John was written so that people would believe that Jesus is the Christ, the Son of God, and that people would have life in him (John 20:31). John 1:1–18 is John's Christmas story and is an introduction to the entire Gospel of John. Compare Matthew 1:18–25 and John 1:1–18, looking for truths in John 1:1–18 that are related to Matthew 1:18–25. Consider these:

- The eternal nature of God includes the Son (John 1:1–2)

- The eternal nature of God came to earth to save people, to help them become children of God (John 1:12)

- The eternal nature of God came to earth in a human being (John 1:14)

A VOICE IN THE NIGHT

What if God made an angelic visit to you? How would you respond if you heard:

- Fear not, I want your child to be dedicated to my service, and you will need to prepare your child for that.

- Fear not, I am working in the life of an outrageous person in your community, and I need you to extend God's grace and love to this person, including sharing with this person how to become a Christian.

- Fear not, act in love toward _____, even though you have trouble understanding what is going on in that person's life right now.

QUESTIONS

1. When angels dealt with Joseph and Mary, fear is mentioned in each case. What kind of fear might Joseph and Mary have had?

2. What are some qualities of a righteous person?

3. How would you have reacted to Mary's story that she was pregnant and God did it?

4. What if someone asked you, *Who is Jesus, and what does he mean to you?* How would you answer them?

5. What can you do differently this Christmas to make sure that Jesus is more central to your celebration of Christmas?

NOTES ———————————————————————————

1. Unless otherwise indicated, all Scripture quotations in the Christmas lesson are from the New International Version.

Our Next New Study
(Available for use beginning March 2011)

THE GOSPEL OF JOHN:
Light Overcoming Darkness

PART TWO—THE LIGHT OVERCOMES (JOHN 13—21)

Additional Resources for Studying the Gospel of John

George R. Beasley-Murray. *John*. Word Biblical Commentary. Volume 36. Second edition. Waco, Texas: Word Books, Publisher, 1999.

Raymond E. Brown. *The Gospel According to John (I—XII)*. Garden City, New York: Doubleday & Company, Inc., 1966.

Raymond E. Brown. *The Gospel According to John (XIII—XXI)*. Garden City, New York: Doubleday & Company, Inc., 1970.

F.F. Bruce. *The Gospel of John*. Grand Rapids, Michigan: William B. Eerdmans Publishing Company, 1983.

Gary M. Burge, *The NIV Application Commentary: John*. Grand Rapids, Michigan: Zondervan Publishing House, 2000.

James E. Carter. *John*. Layman's Bible Book Commentary. Volume 18. Nashville: Broadman Press, 1984.

Herschel H. Hobbs. *The Gospel of John: Invitation to Life*. Nashville, Tennessee: Convention Press, 1988.

William E. Hull. "John." *The Broadman Bible Commentary*. Volume 9. Nashville, Tennessee: Broadman Press, 1970.

Craig S. Keener. *The Gospel of John: A Commentary*. Two volumes. Peabody, Massachusetts: Hendrickson Publishers, 2003.

Lesslie Newbigin. *The Light Has Come: An Exposition of the Fourth Gospel.* Grand Rapids, Michigan: William B. Eerdmans Publishing Company, 1982.

Gail R. O'Day. "The Gospel of John." *The New Interpreter's Bible.* Volume IX. Nashville, Tennessee: Abingdon Press, 1995.

Additional Future Adult Bible Studies

Profiles in Character   For use beginning May 22, 2011
The Corinthian Letters For use beginning September 2011

How to Order More Bible Study Materials

It's easy! Just fill in the following information. For additional Bible study materials available both in print and online, see www.baptistwaypress.org, or get a complete order form of available print materials—including Spanish materials—by calling 1-866-249-1799 or e-mailing baptistway@texasbaptists.org.

Title of item	Price	Quantity	Cost
This Issue:			
The Gospel of John: Light Overcoming Darkness, Part One—Study Guide (BWP001104)	$3.55	_____	_____
The Gospel of John: Light Overcoming Darkness, Part One—Large Print Study Guide (BWP001105)	$3.95	_____	_____
The Gospel of John: Light Overcoming Darkness, Part One—Teaching Guide (BWP001106)	$4.50	_____	_____
Additional Issues Available:			
Growing Together in Christ—Study Guide (BWP001036)	$3.25	_____	_____
Growing Together in Christ—Teaching Guide (BWP001038)	$3.75	_____	_____
Living Faith in Daily Life—Study Guide (BWP001095)	$3.55	_____	_____
Living Faith in Daily Life—Large Print Study Guide (BWP001096)	$3.95	_____	_____
Living Faith in Daily Life—Teaching Guide (BWP001097)	$4.25	_____	_____
Participating in God's Mission—Study Guide (BWP001077)	$3.55	_____	_____
Participating in God's Mission—Large Print Study Guide (BWP001078)	$3.95	_____	_____
Participating in God's Mission—Teaching Guide (BWP001079)	$3.95	_____	_____
Genesis: People Relating to God—Study Guide (BWP001088)	$2.35	_____	_____
Genesis: People Relating to God—Large Print Study Guide (BWP001089)	$2.75	_____	_____
Genesis: People Relating to God—Teaching Guide (BWP001090)	$2.95	_____	_____
Genesis 12—50: Family Matters—Study Guide (BWP000034)	$1.95	_____	_____
Genesis 12—50: Family Matters—Teaching Guide (BWP000035)	$2.45	_____	_____
Leviticus, Numbers, Deuteronomy—Study Guide (BWP000053)	$2.35	_____	_____
Leviticus, Numbers, Deuteronomy—Large Print Study Guide (BWP000052)	$2.35	_____	_____
Leviticus, Numbers, Deuteronomy—Teaching Guide (BWP000054)	$2.95	_____	_____
1 and 2 Samuel—Study Guide (BWP000002)	$2.35	_____	_____
1 and 2 Samuel—Large Print Study Guide (BWP000001)	$2.35	_____	_____
1 and 2 Samuel—Teaching Guide (BWP000003)	$2.95	_____	_____
1 and 2 Kings: Leaders and Followers—Study Guide (BWP001025)	$2.95	_____	_____
1 and 2 Kings: Leaders and Followers Large Print Study Guide (BWP001026)	$3.15	_____	_____
1 and 2 Kings: Leaders and Followers Teaching Guide (BWP001027)	$3.45	_____	_____
Ezra, Haggai, Zechariah, Nehemiah, Malachi—Study Guide (BWP001071)	$3.25	_____	_____
Ezra, Haggai, Zechariah, Nehemiah, Malachi—Large Print Study Guide (BWP001072)	$3.55	_____	_____
Ezra, Haggai, Zechariah, Nehemiah, Malachi—Teaching Guide (BWP001073)	$3.75	_____	_____
Job, Ecclesiastes, Habakkuk, Lamentations—Study Guide (BWP001016)	$2.75	_____	_____
Job, Ecclesiastes, Habakkuk, Lamentations—Large Print Study Guide (BWP001017)	$2.85	_____	_____
Job, Ecclesiastes, Habakkuk, Lamentations—Teaching Guide (BWP001018)	$3.25	_____	_____
Psalms and Proverbs—Study Guide (BWP001000)	$2.75	_____	_____
Psalms and Proverbs—Teaching Guide (BWP001002)	$3.25	_____	_____
Matthew: Hope in the Resurrected Christ—Study Guide (BWP001066)	$3.25	_____	_____
Matthew: Hope in the Resurrected Christ—Large Print Study Guide (BWP001067)	$3.55	_____	_____
Matthew: Hope in the Resurrected Christ—Teaching Guide (BWP001068)	$3.75	_____	_____
Mark: Jesus' Works and Words—Study Guide (BWP001022)	$2.95	_____	_____
Mark: Jesus' Works and Words—Large Print Study Guide (BWP001023)	$3.15	_____	_____
Mark:Jesus' Works and Words—Teaching Guide (BWP001024)	$3.45	_____	_____
Jesus in the Gospel of Mark—Study Guide (BWP000066)	$1.95	_____	_____
Jesus in the Gospel of Mark—Teaching Guide (BWP000067)	$2.45	_____	_____
Luke: Journeying to the Cross—Study Guide (BWP000057)	$2.35	_____	_____
Luke: Journeying to the Cross—Large Print Study Guide (BWP000056)	$2.35	_____	_____
Luke: Journeying to the Cross—Teaching Guide (BWP000058)	$2.95	_____	_____
The Gospel of John: The Word Became Flesh—Study Guide (BWP001008)	$2.75	_____	_____
The Gospel of John: The Word Became Flesh—Large Print Study Guide (BWP001009)	$2.85	_____	_____
The Gospel of John: The Word Became Flesh—Teaching Guide (BWP001010)	$3.25	_____	_____
Acts: Toward Being a Missional Church—Study Guide (BWP001013)	$2.75	_____	_____
Acts: Toward Being a Missional Church—Large Print Study Guide (BWP001014)	$2.85	_____	_____
Acts: Toward Being a Missional Church—Teaching Guide (BWP001015)	$3.25	_____	_____
Romans: What God Is Up To—Study Guide (BWP001019)	$2.95	_____	_____
Romans: What God Is Up To—Large Print Study Guide (BWP001020)	$3.15	_____	_____
Romans: What God Is Up To—Teaching Guide (BWP001021)	$3.45	_____	_____
Galatians and 1&2 Thessalonians—Study Guide (BWP001080)	$3.55	_____	_____
Galatians and 1&2 Thessalonians—Large Print Study Guide (BWP001081)	$3.95	_____	_____
Galatians and 1&2 Thessalonians—Teaching Guide (BWP001082)	$3.95	_____	_____

Ephesians, Philippians, Colossians—Study Guide (BWP001060)	$3.25	____ ____
Ephesians, Philippians, Colossians—Large Print Study Guide (BWP001061)	$3.55	____ ____
Ephesians, Philippians, Colossians—Teaching Guide (BWP001062)	$3.75	____ ____
1, 2 Timothy, Titus, Philemon—Study Guide (BWP000092)	$2.75	____ ____
1, 2 Timothy, Titus, Philemon—Large Print Study Guide (BWP000091)	$2.85	____ ____
1, 2 Timothy, Titus, Philemon—Teaching Guide (BWP000093)	$3.25	____ ____
Letters of James and John—Study Guide (BWP001101)	$3.55	____ ____
Letters of James and John—Large Print Study Guide (BWP001102)	$3.95	____ ____
Letters of James and John—Teaching Guide (BWP001103)	$4.25	____ ____
Revelation—Study Guide (BWP000084)	$2.35	____ ____
Revelation—Large Print Study Guide (BWP000083)	$2.35	____ ____
Revelation—Teaching Guide (BWP000085)	$2.95	____ ____

Coming for use beginning March 2011

The Gospel of John: Light Overcoming Darkness,
Part Two—Study Guide (BWP001109) — $3.55 ____ ____

The Gospel of John: Light Overcoming Darkness,
Part Two—Large Print Study Guide (BWP001110) — $3.95 ____ ____

The Gospel of John: Light Overcoming Darkness,
Part Two—Teaching Guide (BWP001111) — $4.50 ____

Standard (UPS/Mail) Shipping Charges*			
Order Value	Shipping charge**	Order Value	Shipping charge**
$.01—$9.99	$6.50	$160.00—$199.99	$22.00
$10.00—$19.99	$8.00	$200.00—$249.99	$26.00
$20.00—$39.99	$9.00	$250.00—$299.99	$28.00
$40.00—$59.99	$10.00	$300.00—$349.99	$32.00
$60.00—$79.99	$11.00	$350.00—$399.99	$40.00
$80.00—$99.99	$12.00	$400.00—$499.99	$48.00
$100.00—$129.99	$14.00	$500.00—$599.99	$58.00
$130.00—$159.99	$18.00	$600.00—$799.99	$70.00**

Cost
of items (Order value) ____

Shipping charges
(see chart*) ____

TOTAL ____

*Plus, applicable taxes for individuals and other taxable entities (not churches) within Texas will be added. Please call 1-866-249-1799 if the exact amount is needed prior to ordering.

**For order values $800.00 and above, please call 1-866-249-1799 or check www.baptistwaypress.org

Please allow three weeks for standard delivery. For express shipping service: Call 1-866-249-1799 for information on additional charges.

YOUR NAME

PHONE

YOUR CHURCH

DATE ORDERED

SHIPPING ADDRESS

CITY

STATE   ZIP CODE

E-MAIL

MAIL this form with your check for the total amount to
BAPTISTWAY PRESS, Baptist General Convention of Texas,
333 North Washington, Dallas, TX 75246-1798
(Make checks to "Baptist Executive Board.")

OR, **FAX** your order anytime to: 214-828-5376, and we will bill you.

OR, **CALL** your order toll-free: 1-866-249-1799
(M-Th 8:30 a.m.-6:00 p.m.; Fri 8:30 a.m.-5:00 p.m. central time),
and we will bill you.

OR, **E-MAIL** your order to our internet e-mail address:
baptistway@texasbaptists.org, and we will bill you.

OR, **ORDER ONLINE** at www.baptistwaypress.org.

We look forward to receiving your order! Thank you!